2005 SUPPLEMEN

CASES AND MATERIALS

ON

TRADE REGULATION

By

ROBERT PITOFSKY
Sheehy Professor of Law,
Georgetown University Law Center

HARVEY J. GOLDSCHMID
Dwight Professor of Law,
Columbia University School of Law

DIANE P. WOOD
Circuit Judge, U.S. Court of Appeals,
Seventh Circuit;
Senior Lecturer in Law,
University of Chicago Law School

FIFTH EDITION

New York, New York
FOUNDATION PRESS
2005

© 2004 FOUNDATION PRESS
© 2005 By FOUNDATION PRESS
        395 Hudson Street
        New York, NY 10014
        Phone Toll Free 1–877–888–1330
        Fax (212) 367–6799
        fdpress.com
Printed in the United States of America

ISBN 1–58778–842–X

 *TEXT IS PRINTED ON 10% POST CONSUMER RECYCLED PAPER*

TABLE OF CONTENTS

CHAPTER 1: OBJECTIVES AND ORIGINS OF ANTITRUST LAW

Replace last paragraph, page 17, and all of pages 18 to the middle of page 21.

In order to understand the nature of European Union (EU) antitrust law, or competition law as it is referred to in Europe, it is helpful to look at the broad outline of the EU's system of governance. There are now five principal institutions in the Union: the European Parliament, the Council of the European Union,[1] the European Commission, the European Court of Justice, and the European Court of Auditors. The most important non-judicial organ is the Council of the European Union, or the Council of Ministers as it is often called. The Council, according to Article 203 (ex Article 146) of the Rome Treaty,[2] is composed of ministers representing each Member State,

---

[1] The Council of the European Union should not be confused with the European Council and the Council of Europe. The European Council brings together the European heads of state or government and the President of the European Commission but is not a legal council of the EU. See http://ue.eu.int/faqHomePage.asp?nodeIDx=2&command=update. The Council of Europe is an international organization comprised of both EU and non-EU members based in Strasbourg, France. Its primary focus since its inception in 1949 has been on developing a social agenda within Europe. For more information, see http://www.coe.int.

[2] The European Economic Community was established by the Rome Treaty in 1957. The Rome Treaty has been amended several times since then, and the subsequent amendments, along with the initial text, have now been consolidated into a continuously updated version. The current version of the Rome Treaty is referred to as the "Treaty Establishing the European Community." Following a major amendment by the 1997 Treaty of Amsterdam, the previously used numbering of treaty provisions has been changed as well. To avoid confusion, we will refer to both the former and the new article references, as is customarily done.

including representatives from each of the ten new Member States.[3] If the question before the Council is a general one, it is usually composed of the foreign ministers of the twenty-five Member States, but if it is a specialized question, such as agriculture or finance, the ministers with the relevant portfolios will be in attendance. So constituted, the Council functions both as a head of state for the Union and as its chief legislative body.

The Commission in Brussels is the Union's administrative and executive arm. It now has 30 members,[4] which, according to Article 213 (ex Article 157) of the Treaty of Rome, are chosen on the grounds of general competence and independence (although in practice are also allocated carefully among Member States). The Commission is divided into various Directorates-General with responsibility for substantive areas within the Union's competence. The Competition Directorate General, or DG Comp, is responsible for competition policy and enforcement.

The European Court of Justice (ECJ) and the Court of First Instance (CFI), both located in Luxembourg, constitute the Union's judicial branch. The ECJ's function is to review formal decisions of the Commission and to review questions of EC law referred to it by the national courts of the Member States. Since 1988, the ECJ has been assisted by the Court of First Instance, which was established by the Council pursuant to authority granted under Article 225 (ex

---

[3] On May 1, 2004, the European Union underwent the largest expansion in history. There were fifteen Member States prior to the enlargement: Austria, Belgium, Denmark, Finland, France, Germany, Greece, Ireland, Italy, Luxembourg, the Netherlands, Portugal, Spain, Sweden, and the United Kingdom. The enlargement brought ten new countries into the EU: Cyprus, Czech Republic, Estonia, Hungary, Latvia, Lithuania, Malta, Poland, Slovakia, and Slovenia. Bulgaria, Romania, and Turkey are on the list of candidates to join. See http://europa.eu.int/comm/enlargement/enlargement.htm.

[4] See http://europa.eu.int/comm/commissioners/index_en.htm.

Article 168a) of the Treaty of Rome.[5] The CFI has always had jurisdiction over competition cases. Over time, its authority has expanded. It currently also has jurisdiction to rule in the first instance on (1) all actions for annulment, for failure to act, and for damages brought by natural or legal persons against the Community, (2) actions brought against the Commission under the ECSC Treaty by business firms or associations, and (3) disputes between the Community and its officials and employees. The Treaty of Amsterdam, which entered into force on May 1, 1999, contemplates that the Court of First Instance may eventually have jurisdiction over all categories of cases now within the jurisdiction of the Court of Justice except for preliminary references from the national courts made pursuant to Article 234 (ex Article 177) of the Treaty.

Two principles developed by the ECJ make EU competition law of particular importance: first, the Court has held that it has "direct effect" on individuals and companies, which means that violations can be prosecuted without regard to any measures in national law that may apply; second, the Court has developed an equivalent to the Supremacy Clause of the U.S. Constitution, under which EU competition law has primacy over conflicting Member State legislation.

The European Parliament has been gaining power over the years, but it is still misleading to think of it as the counterpart to the British Parliament, the French Assemblé Nationale, or the German Bundestag. Since 1979, members of the Parliament have been elected directly by European voters. The Parliament sits in Strasbourg, France. Its most important role now is to review legislative proposals from the Council and the Commission. If it approves such a proposal, the Council may then enact the proposal by qualified majority; if it does not, or if it is not consulted, then the Council must act unanimously. The Parliament also has the power to put questions to the Commission, which must be answered, and it reviews the Commission's annual general report.

---

[5] Article 225 (ex Article 168a) was added by the Single European Act of 1987, which amended the Rome Treaty in a number of significant respects.

The last institution, the Court of Auditors, was introduced by the Maastricht Treaty. It is responsible for examining the accounts of all revenue and expenditure of the Union and its various constituent bodies, and reporting to both the Parliament and the Council.

Through this elaborate set of institutions, the Union has developed one of the most sophisticated bodies of competition law in the world. When the original Treaty of Rome, which established the European Economic Community, was signed on March 25, 1957, it included as one of its fundamental goals "the institution of a system ensuring that competition in the common market is not distorted."[6] Part Three, Title I, Chapter 1 of the Treaty implemented that goal by setting forth rules on competition that would apply to "undertakings" (Eurospeak for business entities and governments).[7] Article 81 (ex Article 85 – a point not repeated further in this note) of the Rome Treaty prohibits agreements and other concerted practices that have as their object or effect the prevention, restriction, or distortion of competition, unless the European Commission finds that the particular agreement should be exempted from the prohibition because of its beneficial effects. (You should note that the extent to which the beneficial effects must relate to efficiencies, as contrasted with effects on employment, regional development, or other industrial policy goals, has been debated for years within European circles.) Article 82 (ex Article 86) of the Treaty prohibits abuses of a dominant position. Article 86 (ex Article 90) seeks to place state operated monopolies or enterprises with special privileges under the competition regime, to

---

[6]   298 UNTS 11.

[7]   More specifically, "undertakings" as used by Article 81 and 82 refers to "every entity engaged in an economic activity, regardless of the legal status of the entity and the way it is financed." Case C-41/90, Höfner & Elser v. Macrotron, 1991, ECR I-1979, at para 17. This broad definition includes business entities, governmental entities, individuals, and even Member States. Robert Lane, Current Developments – European Union Law, 53 Int'l & Comp. L.Q. 465 (2004).

the greatest extent possible. Finally, Article 87 (ex Article 92) declares that governmental subsidies that distort or threaten to distort competition within the common market are incompatible with it. The Commission is responsible for reviewing state aids, as they are called, and it has the power to require that incompatible aids must be discontinued.

EU competition law underwent significant changes though two sets of regulations and notices that went into effect on May 1, 2004, on the same date as the accession of the ten new Member States. The first set consists of regulations and guidelines that affect the handling of competition claims in the EU, and is commonly referred to as the "modernisation package."[8] The second set, referred to as the "merger review package," incorporates regulations, guidelines and internal reforms to change the process of merger review.[9] Both packages are primarily procedural reforms and, with exception of an important definitional change in the new merger regulation, have little effect on the substantive law.

On December 16, 2002, the member states of the EU agreed on fundamental reforms of Council Regulation 17 and enacted Regulation 1/2003, the first regulation of the modernisation package.[10] Before this regulation went into force on May 1, 2004, the Commission maintained sole discretion over all exemption determinations under Article 81(3). In some cases, the Commission granted individual exemptions, which often were accompanied by significant conditions, and in other cases it issued so-called "block

---

[8] Commission Finalizes Modernization of the EU Antitrust Enforcement Rules, IP/04/411, at http://europa.eu.int/rapid/pressReleasesAction.do?reference=IP/04/411&format=HTML&aged=0&language=EN&guiLanguage=en.

[9] Merger Control: Merger Review Package in a Nutshell, at http://europa.eu.int/comm/competition/publications/special/3_merger.pdf.

[10] Council Reg. (EC) 1/2003, 2003 O.J. (L 1) 1.

exemptions," which exempted certain classes of agreements, determinations and procedures that the Commission deemed consistent with Article 81. In order to make this centralized system work, the Commission required undertakings to file "notifications" with it, pursuant to Article 81(1) and Regulation 17. Those notifications included extensive information from undertakings about pending agreements, decisions and practices.[11] Under the Regulation 17 system, undertakings were permitted to request an advance opinion from the Commission about whether these agreements, decisions and practices were lawful under Article 81(1).[12] Companies that believed their actions to be consistent with Article 81 often chose not to notify (although this was a bit risky, since a wrong guess led to a finding that their agreement was void under Article 81(2), but if an undertaking wanted an exemption under Article 81(3), it had no choice but to notify.[13]

Regulation 1/2003 now grants national competition authorities of Member States ("NCAs")[14] the authority to apply Articles 81 and 82 in full. In practical terms, this means that the Commission no longer has a monopoly over exemption determinations under Article 81(3). The Commission will continue to issue block exemptions, but neither the Commission nor the NCAs are required to uphold block exemptions when they lead to effects that are incompatible with

---

[11] See Council Reg. (EEC) 17/62. See generally Barry Hawk, Common Market and International Antitrust—A Comparative Guide (ed.); Richard Whish, Competition Law, ch. 9 (3d ed. 1993); Leonard Ritter, Francis Rawlinson, and W. David Braun, EC Competition Law—A Practitioner's Guide (Kluwer 1991).

[12] Council Reg. (EEC) 17, art. 2, 1962 O.J. P 13.

[13] Council Reg. (EEC) 17, arts. 4-5, 1962 O.J. P 13.

[14] Commission Notice on Cooperation Within the Network of Competition Authorities, at para 1, 2004 O.J. (C 101) 03, 43.

Article 81(3).[15]   National courts will now make Article 81(3) exemption determinations on a case-by-case basis. This system is expected to increase the number of private EU competition law actions in national courts, because undertakings can no longer use as a delay tactic Article 81(3) defenses that required the Commission's involvement.[16]   Regulation 1/2003 also abolishes the centralized notification system, recognizing that this system imposed considerable cost on undertakings and detracted from the Commission's ability to focus on more serious infringements. [17]

NCAs may bring actions against undertakings when the NCAs are "well placed" to deal with competition law cases.[18] Single NCAs are normally well placed when the challenged practice substantially affects competition predominately in the Member State's territory.[19] NCAs may undertake parallel actions against an agreement or practice when it substantially affects competition within the territories of each respective Member State and an action by one NCA is not likely to

---

[15]   Council Reg. (EC) 1/2003, "Whereas", para 10, 2003 O.J. (L 1) 1; id., art. 29(1); see Robert Lane, Current Developments – European Union Law, 53 Int'l & Comp. L.Q. 465 (2004).

[16]   See Opinion: Rhodri Thompson Q and Kieron Beal, Matrix Chambers, The Lawyer, May 3, 2004, at 17; Donncadh Woods, The Growth of Private Rights of Action Outside the U.S.: Private Enforcement of Antitrust Rules – Modernization of the EU Rules and the Road Ahead, 16 Loy. Consumer L. Rev. 431, 433 (2004).

[17]   Council Reg. (EC) 1/2003, "Whereas," paras 1-4, 2003 O.J. (L 1) 1.

[18]   Commission Notice on Cooperation Within the Network of Competition Authorities, at paras 8-10, 2004 O.J. (C 101) 03, 43.

[19]   Council Reg. (EC) 1/2003, art. 6, 2003 O.J. (L 1) 1; Commission Notice on Cooperation Within the Network of Competition Authorities, at para 10, 2004 O.J. (C 101) 03, 43.

bring about an end to the offense.[20] As before, NCAs are prohibited from applying national competition laws that conflict with Articles 81 and 82, unless applying national merger control laws or national law that falls entirely outside the domain of competition law as reflected in Articles 81 and 82.[21] Under this system of parallel competences, the Commission retains jurisdiction over all EU competition law cases and a decision by the Commission to initiate proceedings destroys the competence of Member States to apply Articles 81 and 82 unless the case is in the process of appellate review at a national court.[22]

Everyone involved in these reforms recognizes that to allow multiple competition authorities to investigate and instigate proceedings against an undertaking is at the same time to run the risk of wasteful or harassing multiple investigations and actions against an undertaking for the same offense. To guard against this possibility and to decrease duplication and waste in multiple enforcement, the regulations and guidelines provide that when one NCA is dealing with an Article 81 or 82 case, other NCAs may suspend the proceedings before them or reject the complaint and the Commission may refuse to initiate proceedings.[23] The regulations and guidelines also protect the information collected from undertakings. The Commission and NCAs are under an obligation not to disclose (other than in accordance with the rules of the proceeding) information "covered by the obligation of professional secrecy," which includes business secrets and other confidential information.[24] Information exchanged

---

[20] Commission Notice on Cooperation Within the Network of Competition Authorities, at para 12, 2004 O.J. (C 101) 03, 43.

[21] Council Reg. (EC) 1/2003, art. 3(1-3), 2003 O.J. (L 1) 1

[22] Council Reg. (EC) 1/2003, art. 11(6), 2003 O.J. (L 1) 1; id., art. 35(3).

[23] Council Reg. (EC) 1/2003, art. 13, 2003 O.J. (L 1) 1.

[24] Council Reg. (EC) 1/2003, art. 28, 2003 O.J. (L 1) 1; Commission Notice on Cooperation Within the Network of Competition Authorities, at para 28(a), 2004 O.J. (C 101) 03, 43.

between NCAs and the Commission may be used only for applying Articles 81 and 82 and parallel national competition law so long as the national competition law does not lead to an outcome inconsistent with Articles 81 and 82.[25] The information exchanged among NCAs and the Commission also may not be used to impose sanctions greater than permissible under the laws of the Member State of the transferring authority.[26]

While the procedural reform package decentralizes the adjudication of competition law claims, it would be a mistake to think that this necessarily means that, from a procedural standpoint, EU competition law will now evolve into something resembling the law of the United States. First, the Commission will continue to handle infringements involving Community-wide effects on competition by virtue of being well placed to handle such cases. The Commission has gone so far as to issue a notice announcing that it is best placed to initiate proceedings when agreements or practices have effects on competition in more than three Member States.[27] Second, and more importantly, the new regulations and guidelines actively seek to minimize the number of conflicting decisions. The courts of Member States may not decide an Article 81 or 82 case in a way that runs counter to a decision adopted by the Commission on the same subject.[28] At least 30 days prior to the adoption of a decision by a

---

[25] Council Reg. (EC) 1/2003, art. 12(2), 2003 O.J. (L 1) 1; Commission Notice on Cooperation Within the Network of Competition Authorities, at para 28(b), 2004 O.J. (C 101) 03, 43.

[26] Council Reg. (EC) 1/2003, art. 12(3), 2003 O.J. (L 1) 1; Commission Notice on Cooperation Within the Network of Competition Authorities, at para 28(c), 2004 O.J. (C 101) 03, 43.

[27] Commission Notice on Cooperation Within the Network of Competition Authorities, at para 14, 2004 O.J. (C 101) 03, 43.

[28] Council Reg. (EC) 1/2003, art. 16, 2003 O.J. (L 1) 1; Commission Notice on Cooperation Within the Network of Competition Authorities, at para 43, 2004 O.J. (C 101) 03, 43. (It remains to be seen how tightly the European courts and the Commission will

Footnote continued on next page

national court, the NCA of that Member State must inform the Commission and provide a summary of the case and the proposed decision.[29]   This period will allow the Commission to assess the proposed decision and, in the process, the Commission may communicate with the NCA to ensure consistent application of Community law.[30]   So long as the Commission does not institute proceedings, the decision will become adopted after the expiration of the 30-day period.[31]

A more recent push in EU competition law has resulted in the replacement of the original merger regulation[32] with a new one (the "EC Merger Regulation").[33]   The new regulation came into force on May 1, 2004. Like the previous merger regulation, the new regulation requires undertakings to notify the Commission pending certain combinations and joint ventures, or "concentrations," having

---

Footnote continued from previous page
construe this obligation. One could imagine a rule in which the national authorities are bound only if a new case has arisen out of the very same subject matter of the previous case. Alternatively, and perhaps more likely in view of the need to develop a consistent body of law, the rule might be construed to require national courts to follow Commission decisions applicable to a class of agreements, decisions or practices.)

[29]   Council Reg. (EC) 1/2003, art. 11(4), 2003 O.J. (L 1) 1; Commission Notice on Cooperation Within the Network of Competition Authorities, at para 46, 2004 O.J. (C 101) 03, 43.

[30]   Commission Notice on Cooperation Within the Network of Competition Authorities, at para 46, 2004 O.J. (C 101) 03, 43.

[31]   Commission Notice on Cooperation Within the Network of Competition Authorities, at para 1, 2004 O.J. (C 101) 03, 46.

[32]   Council Reg. (EEC) 4064/89, 1989 O.J. (L 395).

[33]   Council Reg. (EC) 139/2004, 2004 O.J. (L 24) 1.

"Community dimension."[34]   A concentration results when two previously independent undertakings combine or when a person who controls one undertaking acquires another undertaking.[35]   These concentrations have community dimension when they involve a worldwide turnover of 5 billion Euros and for which the intra-Community turnover is 250 million Euros for each of at least two participants, as long as more than two-thirds of the intra-Community turnover is not in one and the same Member State.[36]   Concentrations may also have a community dimension when they involve worldwide turnover of 2.5 billion Euros, turnover of more than 100 million Euros in each of at least three Member States and more than 25 million in at least two of those three, and at least two undertakings each having turnover of at least 100 million Euros, so long as more than two-thirds of aggregate intra-Community turnover is not within one Member State.[37]   Other concentrations are reviewed at the Member State level, subject to the possibility of centralized review as discussed below.

Compared to modernisation package, the merger control package makes modest, but important substantive, jurisdictional, and structural modifications to the merger control system.[38]   Article 82 prohibits any abuse by a single undertaking or a group of undertakings holding a "dominant position" in a market of the European Community.   The EC Merger Regulation changes the emphasis of the substantive test used to determine whether an undertaking or a group of undertakings holds a dominant position. While the substantive test remains largely the same, the new test focuses on the effects a concentration has on competition instead of

---

[34]   Council Reg. (EC) 139/2004, art. 1(1), 2004 O.J. (L 24) 1.

[35]   Council Reg. (EC) 139/2004, art. 3(1), 2004 O.J. (L 24) 1.

[36]   Council Reg. (EC) 139/2004, art. 1(2), 2004 O.J. (L 24) 1.
[37]   Council Reg. (EC) 139/2004, art. 1(3), 2004 O.J. (L 24) 1.

[38]   Merger Control: Merger Review Package in a Nutshell, at http://europa.eu.int/comm/competition/publications/special/3_merger.pdf.

focusing on the creation or strengthening of a dominant position of one or more undertakings.[39] The new regulation also adds a reference to oligopolies in the preamble to make clear that oligopolies are indeed covered by the regulation.[40] The Commission expects that these two modifications will end a long-standing debate over whether oligopolies (or coordinated effects cases, as they are sometimes called, as opposed to unilateral effects cases) are covered under the "dominant position" language of Article 82.[41]

---

[39] Compare Council Reg. (EEC) 4064/89, art. 2(3), 1989 O.J. (L 395) ("A concentration which creates or strengthens a dominant position as a result of which effective competition would be significantly impeded in the common market or in a substantial part of it shall be declared incompatible with the common market.") with Council Reg. (EC) 139/2004, art. 2(3), 2004 O.J. (L 24) 1. ("A concentration which would significantly impede effective competition, in the common market or in a substantial part of it, in particular as a result of the creation or strengthening of a dominant position, shall be declared incompatible with the common market."). See Merger Control: Merger Review Package in a Nutshell, at http://europa.eu.int/comm/competition/publications/ special/3_merger.pdf.

[40] Council Reg. (EC) 139/2004, "Whereas," para 25, 2004 O.J. (L 24) 1; Robert Lane, Current Developments – European Union Law, 53.2 Int'l & Comp. L.Q. 465 (2004).

[41] Merger Control: Merger Review Package in a Nutshell, at http://europa.eu.int/comm/competition/publications/special/3_merger. pdf; New Merger Reg. Frequently Asked Questions, MEMO/04/9, at http://europa.eu.int/rapid/pressReleasesAction.do?reference=IP/04/70 &format=HTML&aged=0&language=EN&guiLanguage=en. Oligopolies have historically posed a special problem to the Commission's application of Article 82 because oligopolies are not "dominant" in the sense that they are much larger than competitors. By adjusting the definition of dominance to focus on the concentrations that threaten competition and including a reference to oligopolies in the preamble, the new regulation sweeps oligopolies under the purview of the merger control system.

The EC Merger Regulation increases the time period within which merger review may take place, in order to add more flexibility to the system. The new time periods ensure that mergers are not blocked because undertakings do not have sufficient time to discuss remedies with the Commission.[42] Under the new regulation, the deadline for the end of the first phase of a merger review was increased from one month to twenty-five working days, with an extension of an additional ten working days for referral requests.[43] The deadline for the end of the second phase was increased from four months to ninety working days, again with the possibility of extension.[44]

While the modernisation package decentralizes the adjudication of competition claims, the merger control package reinforces a "one-stop shop" concept for reviewing concentrations lacking Community dimension. The former merger regulation was introduced after years of debate, in order to give exclusive competence to Brussels over very large concentrations. The thresholds were so high, however, that multiple filings were common, and as more countries enacted their own merger control laws and the Community itself became larger, the problems associated with multiple filings also grew. The new regulation is intended to reduce the number of multiple filings even further by allowing undertakings

---

[42] New Merger Reg. Frequently Asked Questions, MEMO/04/9, at http://europa.eu.int/rapid/pressReleasesAction.do?reference=IP/04/70 &format=HTML&aged=0&language=EN&guiLanguage=en.

[43] Council Reg. (EC) 139/2004, art. 10(1), 2004 O.J. (L 24) 1; see New Merger Reg. Frequently Asked Questions, MEMO/04/9, http://europa.eu.int/rapid/pressReleasesAction.do?reference=IP/04/70 &format=HTML&aged=0&language=EN&guiLanguage=en.

[44] Council Reg. (EC) 139/2004, art. 10(3), 2004 O.J. (L 24) 1; see New Merger Reg. Frequently Asked Questions, MEMO/04/9, at http://europa.eu.int/rapid/pressReleasesAction.do?reference=IP/04/70 &format=HTML&aged=0&language=EN&guiLanguage=en.

that would otherwise have to notify at least three Member States to petition the Commission for a centralized merger review.[45] The Commission will then inform the Member States of the petition and, so long as no member state objects within fifteen days, the Commission will examine the concentration.[46] An undertaking may now petition the Commission to notify a Member State instead of the Commission about a concentration having Community dimension when the concentration will significantly affect competition in a the Member State.[47] These reforms were highly anticipated by the business community because they are expected to reduce costs associated with filing to authorities who would not ultimately perform the review. In addition, undertakings now can notify the Commission when they have a good faith intent to conclude an agreement instead of needing to wait until after they conclude a binding agreement.[48]

Much of the near-explosive spread of competition laws around the world in more recent years reflects both the success and the strong influence of the European Union's competition laws, both taken alone and in combination with those in the Americas and the Asia–Pacific region. Throughout Central and Eastern Europe, countries eager to join the EU one day have modeled their new competition laws on those of the EU, in recognition of the fact that accession would mean the acceptance of the full *acquis communautaire* of competition laws, regulations, and court precedents. In addition, the administrative approach taken by the EC appeals to countries that do not share the Anglo–American common-law tradition. For that reason, we allude from time to time throughout this casebook to European rules, both by way of comparison and contrast. The extent to which European law follows efficiency principles, the extent to which it continues to reflect its roots by giving primacy to intra-European market integration goals, and the extent to which it displays more concern for

---

[45] Council Reg. (EC) 139/2004, art. 4(5), 2004 O.J. (L 24) 1.

[46] Council Reg. (EC) 139/2004, art. 4(5), 2004 O.J. (L 24) 1.

[47] Council Reg. (EC) 139/2004, art. 4(4), 2004 O.J. (L 24) 1.

[48] Council Reg. (EC) 139/2004, art. 4(1), 2004 O.J. (L 24) 1.

equitable market behavior, all provide a useful perspective for our consideration of U.S. law.

As noted above, the central competition provisions of EC law are Articles 81 and 82 of the Rome Treaty. These provisions are set forth below. At this point, please compare Articles 81 and 82 with the provisions of Sections 1 and 2 of the Sherman Act, pp. 14-15 *supra*.

CHAPTER 2: FRAMEWORK OF ANTITRUST POLICY

Replace paragraph 2, page 71, with the following:

In 2004, Congress passed and the President signed the Antitrust Criminal Penalty Enforcement and Reform Act. The statute substantially increased civil and criminal penalties for antitrust violations. Congress' purpose was to make criminal penalties for antitrust offenses more consistent with the harsh penalties for white collar crime established in recent legislation. Criminal proceedings can result in imprisonment of individuals for a maximum of ten years (up from three years previously). Criminal fines for corporations was increased from $10 million to $100 million and criminal fines for individuals was increased from $350,000 to $1 million.

Insert before "INTERVENTION" at page 89:

Largely in response to the 1995 Circuit Court decision in *Microsoft* criticizing a District Judge for refusing to enter a proposed settlement, discussed in the text at pages 88 and 89, and the 2003 district court confirmation of a proposed settlement, Congress sought to clarify that district courts are to undertake a more thorough and independent determination of whether a proposed consent decree is adequate. Congress also changed the directive to the courts from the language that they "may" consider certain factors to "shall" consider those factors. It also changed slightly the language of the Tunney Act mandate (language changes are underscored):

> (a)   The competitive impact of such judgment, including termination of alleged violations, provisions for enforcement and modification, duration or relief sought, anticipated effects of alternative remedies actually considered, whether its terms are ambiguous and other competitive

considerations bearing on the adequacy of such judgment that the court deems necessary to a determination of whether the consent judgment is in the public interest, and

(b)   The impact of entry of such judgment upon competition in the relevant market or markets, upon the public generally and individuals alleging specific injury from the violations set forth in the complaint including consideration of the public benefit, if any, to be derived from a determination of the issues at trial.

CHAPTER 5: GROUP REFUSALS TO DEAL AND JOINT VENTURES

Section 2: Joint Ventures Revisited

Add the following after Note 1, page 398.

In 2003, a unanimous Court of Appeals for the Second Circuit affirmed the District Court opinion. *United States* v. *VISA USA, Inc.,* and *MasterCard International*, 344 F.3d 229 (2nd Cir. 2003). The United States had not appealed its loss in the court below on its challenge to the dual governance market structure. With respect to rules adopted by VISA and MasterCard, and applied to its 20,000 bank members - that a bank could belong to the VISA and MasterCard system but not to other competitive systems (specifically American Express and Discover) - the court found an adverse effect on competition in violation of Section 1. In response to the VISA/MasterCard argument that the arrangement with the banks was like a vertical distributorship that has been seen in other contexts as virtually *per se* legal (*see* casebook, *infra*, at page 931), the court concluded that might be a valid argument if the arrangement was entered into by a single seller. The court concluded however that the 20,000-member banks in effect had entered into a horizontal agreement to exclude American Express and Discover, and that agreement injured not just those two competitors but competition in general.

> "The fact that they harm competitors does not, however, mean they do not also harm competition. . . . VISA USA and MasterCard would be impelled to design and market their products more competitively if the banks to which they sell their services were free to purchase network services from AmEx and Discover." 344 F.3d at 243.

Insert following Notes, p. 402

IMS Health Note

In *IMS Health Inc. v. Commission*, Case T-184/01 (Order of the President of the Court of First Instance of 10 March 2005), competitors of IMS Health ('IMS') sought compulsory licensing of its regional sales data service. A subsidiary of IMS provided information to companies in the pharmaceutical and healthcare product sectors in Germany. The subsidiary based its service on a "brick structure" that divided Germany into geographical zones for reporting data on sales of medicinal products. After a German court ruled that the brick structure warranted copyright protection, two competing pharmaceutical service companies filed an competition complaint with the European Commission, claiming that IMS's refusal to license the brick structure to them was an unfair monopolization of essential facilities that deprived them of the ability to compete with IMS. The Commission agreed and adopted interim measures compelling IMS to license the brick structure to its competitors.

In 2001, IMS challenged the Commission's decision in an action before the European Union's Court of First Instance ('CFI'), claiming that the essential facilities doctrine should not be extended to instances in which a company uses its dominant market position to further its interests only in that market, rather than in ancillary markets. The CFI suspended the application of the Commission's decision until the final resolution of the case. While the case was pending, however, one of the competitors withdrew from the market, while the other gained sufficient market share to enable it to compete without a license to use IMS's brick structure. The Commission withdrew its decision following this change in circumstances, and the CFI subsequently dismissed the case, holding that there was no longer a need for it to give a decision on the case.

This means that important questions remain to be resolved about the scope of the essential facilities doctrine that the European courts ultimately will recognize. In the wake of *Verizon Communications, Inc. v. Law Offices of Curtis V. Trinko*, 540 U.S. 398 (2004), similar questions exist about the future of an independent "essential facilities" doctrine in the United States, although it appears

19

in general that the U.S. doctrine will be a narrower one than the European doctrine.

CHAPTER 8: ADDITIONAL LIMITATIONS ON A SINGLE FIRM

Insert after *Aspen Skiing*, page 750.

VERIZON COMMUNICATIONS v. LAW OFFICE

OF CURTIS V. TRINKO

SUPREME COURT OF THE UNITED STATES, 2004

540 U.S., 398, 124 S. CT., 872, 159, L. ED. 2D 823

SCALIA, J. The Telecommunications Act of 1996, Pub. L. 104-104, 110 Stat. 56, imposes certain duties upon incumbent local telephone companies in order to facilitate market entry by competitors, and establishes a complex regime for monitoring and enforcement. In this case we consider whether a complaint alleging breach of the incumbent's duty under the 1996 Act to share its network with competitors states a claim under §2 of the Sherman Act, 26 Stat. 209.

I

Petitioner Verizon Communications Inc. is the incumbent local exchange carrier (LEC) serving New York State. Before the 1996 Act, Verizon,[49] like other incumbent LECs, enjoyed an exclusive franchise within its local service area. The 1996 Act sought

---

[49] In 1996, NYNEX was the incumbent LEC for New York State. NYNEX subsequently merged with Bell Atlantic Corporation, and the merged entity retained the Bell Atlantic name; a further merger produced Verizon. We use "Verizon" to refer to NYNEX and Bell Atlantic as well.

to "uproo[t]" the incumbent LECs' monopoly and to introduce competition in its place. *Verizon Communications Inc.* v. *FCC,* 535 U.S. 467, 488 (2002). Central to the scheme of the Act is the incumbent LEC's obligation under 47 U.S.C. §251(c) to share its network with competitors, see *AT&T Corp.* v. *Iowa Utilities Bd.,* 525 U.S. 366, 371 (1999), including provision of access to individual elements of the network on an "unbundled" basis. §251(c)(3). New entrants, so-called competitive LECs, resell these unbundled network elements (UNEs), recombined with each other or with elements belonging to the LECs.

Verizon, like other incumbent LECs, has taken two significant steps within the Act's framework in the direction of increased competition. First, Verizon has signed interconnection agreements with rivals such as AT&T, as it is obliged to do under §252, detailing the terms on which it will make its network elements available. (Because Verizon and AT&T could not agree upon terms, the open issues were subjected to compulsory arbitration under §§252(b) and (c).) In 1997, the state regulator, New York's Public Service Commission (PSC), approved Verizon's interconnection agreement with AT&T.

Second, Verizon has taken advantage of the opportunity provided by the 1996 Act for incumbent LECs to enter the long-distance market (from which they had long been excluded). That required Verizon to satisfy, among other things, a 14-item checklist of statutory requirements, which includes compliance with the Act's network-sharing duties. §§271(d)(3)(A) and (c)(2)(B). Checklist item two, for example, includes "nondiscriminatory access to network elements in accordance with the requirements" of §251(c)(3). §271(c)(2)(B)(ii). Whereas the state regulator approves an interconnection agreement, for long-distance approval the incumbent LEC applies to the Federal Communications Commission (FCC). In December 1999, the FCC approved Verizon's §271 application for New York.

Part of Verizon's UNE obligation under §251(c)(3) is the provision of access to operations support systems (OSS), a set of systems used by incumbent LECs to provide services to customers and ensure quality. Verizon's interconnection agreement and long-

22

distance authorization each specified the mechanics by which its OSS obligation would be met. As relevant here, a competitive LEC sends orders for service through an electronic interface with Verizon's ordering system, and as Verizon completes certain steps in filling the order, it sends confirmation back through the same interface. Without OSS access a rival cannot fill its customers' orders.

In late 1999, competitive LECs complained to regulators that many orders were going unfilled, in violation of Verizon's obligation to provide access to OSS functions. The PSC and FCC opened parallel investigations, which led to a series of orders by the PSC and a consent decree with the FCC.[50] Under the FCC consent decree, Verizon undertook to make a "voluntary contribution" to the U.S. Treasury in the amount of $3 million, 15 FCC Rcd. 5415, 5421, 116 (2000); under the PSC orders, Verizon incurred liability to the competitive LECs in the amount of $10 million. Under the consent decree and orders, Verizon was subjected to new performance measurements and new reporting requirements to the FCC and PSC, with additional penalties for continued noncompliance. In June 2000, the FCC terminated the consent decree. Enforcement Bureau Announces that Bell Atlantic Has Satisfied Consent Decree Regarding Electronic Ordering Systems in New York (June 20, 2000), http://www.fcc.gov/eb/ News_Releases/bellatlet.html (all Internet materials as visited Dec. 12, 2003, and available in the Clerk of Court's case file). The next month the PSC relieved Verizon of the

---

[50] Order Directing Improvements To Wholesale Service Performance, *MCI Worldcom, Inc.* v. *Bell Atlantic-New York*, Nos. 00-C-0008, 00-C-0009, 2000 WL 363378 (N. Y. PSC, Feb. 11, 2000); Order Directing Market Adjustments and Amending Performance Assurance Plan, *MCI Worldcom, Inc.* v. *Bell Atlantic-New York*, Nos. 00-C-0008, 00-C-0009, 99-C-0949, 2000 WL 517633 (N. Y. PSC, Mar. 23, 2000); Order Addressing OSS Issues, *MCI Worldcom, Inc.* v. *Bell Atlantic-New York*, Nos. 00-C-0008, 00-C-0009, 99-C-0949, 2000 WL 1531916 (N.Y. PSC, July 27, 2000); I*n re Bell Atlantic-New York Authorization Under Section 271 of the Communications Act to Provide In-Region, InterLATA Service in the State of New York*, 15 FCC Rcd. 5413 (2000) (Order); *id.,* at 5415 (Consent Decree).

heightened reporting requirement. Order Addressing OSS Issues, *MCI Worldcom, Inc.* v. *Bell Atlantic-New York,* Nos. 00-C-0008, 00-C-0009, 99-C- 0949, 2000 WL 1531916 (N. Y. PSC, July 27, 2000).

Respondent Law Offices of *Curtis V. Trinko, LLP*, a New York City law firm, was a local telephone service customer of AT&T. The day after Verizon entered its consent decree with the FCC, respondent filed a complaint in the District Court for the Southern District of New York, on behalf of itself and a class of similarly situated customers, See App. 12-33. The complaint, as later amended, *id.,* at 34-50, alleged that Verizon had filled rivals' orders on a discriminatory basis as part of an anticompetitive scheme to discourage customers from becoming or remaining customers of competitive LECs, thus impeding the competitive LECs' ability to enter and compete in the market for local telephone service. See, *e.g., id.,* at 34-35, 46-47, §§1, 2, 52, 54. According to the complaint, Verizon "has filled orders of [competitive LEC] customers after filling those for its own local phone service, has failed to fill in a timely manner, or not at all, a substantial number of orders for [competitive LEC] customers . . ., and has systematically failed to inform [competitive LECs] of the status of their customers' orders." *Id.,* at 39, ¶21. The complaint set forth a single example of the alleged "failure to provide adequate access to [competitive LECs]," namely the OSS failure that resulted in the FCC consent decree and PSC orders. *Id.,* at 40, ¶22, It asserted that the result of Verizon's improper "behavior with respect to providing access to its local loop" was to "deter potential customers [of rivals] from switching." *Id.,* at 47, ¶57, 35, ¶2. The complaint sought damages and injunctive relief for violation of §2 of the Sherman Act, 15 U.S.C. §2, pursuant to the remedy provisions of §§4 and 16 of the Clayton Act, 38 Stat. 731, as amended, 15 U.S.C. §15, 26. The complaint also alleged violations of the 1996 Act, §202(a) of the Communications Act of 1934, 48 Stat. 1064, as amended, 47 U.S.C. §151 *et seq.,* and state law.

The District Court dismissed the complaint in its entirety. As to the antitrust portion, it concluded that respondent's allegations of deficient assistance to rivals failed to satisfy the requirements of §2. The Court of Appeals for the Second Circuit reinstated the complaint in part, including the antitrust claim. 305 F. 3d 89, 113 (2002). We granted certiorari, limited to the question whether the Court of

Appeals erred in reversing the District Court's dismissal of respondent's antitrust claims. 538 U.S. 905 (2003).

II

To decide this case, we must first determine what effect (if any) the 1996 Act has upon the application of traditional antitrust principles. The Act imposes a large number of duties upon incumbent LECs — above and beyond those basic responsibilities it imposes upon all carriers, such as assuring number portability and providing access to rights-of-way, see 47 U.S.C. §§251(b)(2), (4). Under the sharing duties of §251(c), incumbent LECs are required to offer three kinds of access. Already noted, and perhaps most intrusive, is the duty to offer access to UNEs on "just, reasonable, and nondiscriminatory" terms, §251(c)(3), a phrase that the FCC has interpreted, to mean a price reflecting long-run incremental cost. See *Verizon Communications Inc.* v. *FCC,* 535 U.S., at 495-496. A rival can interconnect its own facilities with those of the incumbent LEC, or it can simply purchase services at wholesale from the incumbent and resell them to consumers. See §§251(c)(2), (4). The Act also imposes upon incumbents the duty to allow physical "collocation" - that is, to permit a competitor to locate and install its equipment on the incumbent's premises - which makes feasible interconnection and access to UNEs. See §251(c)(6).

That Congress created these duties, however, does not automatically lead to the conclusion that they can be enforced by means of an antitrust claim. Indeed, a detailed regulatory scheme such as that created by the 1996 Act ordinarily raises the question whether the regulated entities are not shielded from antitrust scrutiny altogether by the doctrine of implied immunity. See, *e.g., United States* v. *National Assn. of Securities Dealers, Inc.,* 422 U.S. 694 (1975); *Gordon* v. *New York Stock Exchange, Inc.,* 422 U.S. 659 (1975). In some respects the enforcement scheme set up by the 1996 Act is a good candidate for implication of antitrust immunity, to avoid the real possibility of judgments conflicting with the agency's regulatory scheme "that might be voiced by courts exercising jurisdiction under the antitrust laws." *United States* v. *National Assn. of Securities Dealers, Inc., supra,* at 734.

25

Congress, however, precluded that interpretation. Section 601(b)(l) of the 1996 Act is an antitrust-specific saving clause providing that "nothing in this Act or the amendments made by this Act shall be construed to modify, impair, or supersede the applicability of any of the antitrust laws." 110 Stat. 143, 47 U.S.C. §152, note. This bars a finding of implied immunity. As the FCC has put the point, the saving clause preserves those "claims that satisfy established antitrust standards." Brief for United States and the Federal Communications Commission as *Amici Curiae* Supporting Neither Party in No. 0-7057, *Covad Communications Co.* v. *Bell Atlantic Corp.* (CADC), p. 8.

But just as the 1996 Act preserves claims that satisfy existing antitrust standards, it does not create new claims that go beyond existing antitrust standards; that would be equally inconsistent with the saving clause's mandate that nothing in the Act "modify, impair, or supersede the applicability" of the antitrust laws. We turn, then, to whether the activity of which respondent complains violates preexisting antitrust standards.

III

The complaint alleges that Verizon denied interconnection services to rivals in order to limit entry. If that allegation states an antitrust claim at all, it does so under §2 of the Sherman Act, 15 U.S.C. §2, which declares that a firm shall not "monopolize" or "attempt to monopolize." *Ibid.* It is settled law that this offense requires, in addition to the possession of monopoly power in the relevant market, "the willful acquisition or maintenance of that power as distinguished from growth or development as a consequence of a superior product, business acumen, or historic accident." *United States* v. *Grinnell Corp.,* 384 U.S 563, 570-571 (1966). The mere possession of monopoly power, and the concomitant charging of monopoly prices, is not only not unlawful; it is an important element of the free-market system. The opportunity to charge monopoly prices - at least for a short period - is what attracts "business acumen" in the first place; it induces risk taking that produces innovation and economic growth. To safeguard the incentive to innovate, the possession of monopoly power will not be found unlawful unless it is accompanied by an element of anticompetitive *conduct.*

Firms may acquire monopoly power by establishing an infrastructure that renders them uniquely suited to serve their customers. Compelling such firms to share the source of their advantage is in some tension with the underlying purpose of antitrust law, since it may lessen the incentive for the monopolist, the rival, or both to invest in those economically beneficial facilities. Enforced sharing also requires antitrust courts to act as central planners, identifying the proper price, quantity, and other terms of dealing - a role for which they are ill-suited. Moreover, compelling negotiation between competitors may facilitate the supreme evil of antitrust: collusion. Thus, as a general matter, the Sherman Act "does not restrict the long recognized right of [a] trader or manufacturer engaged in an entirely private business, freely to exercise his own independent discretion as to parties with whom he will deal." *United States* v. *Colgate & Co., 250 U.S. 300, 307 (1919)*.

However, "[t]he high value that we have placed on the right to refuse to deal with other firms does not mean that the right is unqualified." *Aspen Skiing Co.* v. *Aspen Highlands Skiing Corp., 472 U.S. 585, 601 (1985)*. Under certain circumstances, a refusal to cooperate with rivals can constitute anticompetitive conduct and violate §2. We have been very cautious in recognizing such exceptions, because of the uncertain virtue of forced sharing and the difficulty of identifying and remedying anticompetitive conduct by a single firm. The question before us today is whether the allegations of respondent's complaint fit within existing exceptions or provide a basis, under traditional antitrust principles, for recognizing a new one.

The leading case for §2 liability based on refusal to cooperate with a rival, and the case upon which respondent understandably places greatest reliance, is *Aspen Skiing, supra.* The Aspen ski area consisted of four mountain areas. The defendant, who owned three of those areas, and the plaintiff, who owned the fourth, had cooperated for years in the issuance of a joint, multiple-day, all-area ski ticket. After repeatedly demanding an increased share of the proceeds, the defendant canceled the joint ticket. The plaintiff, concerned that skiers would bypass its mountain without some joint offering, tried a variety of increasingly desperate measures to re-create the joint ticket, even to the point of in effect offering to buy the defendant's tickets at retail price. *Id.,* at 593-594. The defendant refused even that. We upheld a jury verdict for the plaintiff, reasoning that "[t]he jury may well have concluded that [the defendant] elected to forgo these short-run benefits because it was more interested in reducing competition . . . over the long run by harming its smaller competitor." *Id.*, at 608.

Aspen Skiing is at or near the outer boundary of §2 liability. The Court there found significance in the defendant's decision to cease participation in a cooperative venture. See *id.*, at 608, 610-611. The unilateral termination of a voluntary *(and thus presumably profitable)* course of dealing suggested a willingness to forsake short-term profits to achieve an anticompetitive end. *Ibid.* Similarly, the defendant's unwillingness to renew the ticket *even if compensated at retail price* revealed a distinctly anticompetitive bent.

The refusal to deal alleged in the present case does not fit within the limited exception recognized in *Aspen Skiing*. The complaint does not allege that Verizon voluntarily engaged in a course of dealing with its rivals, or would ever have done so absent statutory compulsion. Here, therefore, the defendant's prior conduct sheds no light upon the motivation of its refusal to deal - upon whether its regulatory lapses were prompted not by competitive zeal but by anticompetitive malice. The contrast between the cases is heightened by the difference in pricing behavior. In *Aspen Skiing*, the defendant turned down a proposal to sell at its own retail price, suggesting a calculation that its future monopoly retail price would be higher. Verizon's reluctance to interconnect at the cost-based rate of compensation available under §251(c)(3) tells us nothing about dreams of monopoly.

The specific nature of what the 1996 Act compels makes this case different from *Aspen Skiing* in a more fundamental way. In *Aspen Skiing,* what the defendant refused to provide to its competitor was a product that it already sold at retail - to oversimplify slightly, lift tickets representing a bundle of services to skiers. Similarly, in *Otter Tail Power Co.* v. *United States,* 410 U.S. 366 (1973), another case relied upon by respondent, the defendant was already in the business of providing a service to certain customers (power transmission over its network), and refused to provide the same service to certain other customers. *Id.*, at 370-371, 377-378. In the present case, by contrast, the services allegedly withheld are not otherwise marketed or available to the public. The sharing obligation imposed by the 1996 Act created "something brand new" – "the wholesale market for leasing network elements." *Verizon Communications Inc.* v. *FCC,* 535 U.S., at 528. The unbundled elements offered pursuant to §251(c)(3) exist only deep within the bowels of Verizon; they are brought out on compulsion of the 1996 Act and offered not to consumers but to rivals, and at considerable expense and effort. New systems must be designed and implemented simply to make that access possible - indeed, it is the failure of one of those systems that prompted the present complaint.[51]

We conclude that Verizon's alleged insufficient assistance in the provision of service to rivals is not a recognized antitrust claim under this Court's existing refusal-to-deal precedents. This conclusion would be unchanged even if we considered to be established law the "essential facilities" doctrine crafted by some lower courts, under which the Court of Appeals concluded respondent's allegations might state a claim. See generally Areeda, Essential Facilities: An Epithet in Need of Limiting Principles, 58 Antitrust L. J. 841 (1989). We have never recognized such a doctrine, see *Aspen Skiing Co.,* 472 U.S., at 611, n. 44; *AT&T Corp.* v. *Iowa Utilities Bd.,* 525 U.S., at 428 (opinion of BREYER, J.), and we find no need either to recognize it or to repudiate it here. It suffices for present purposes to note that the indispensable requirement for invoking the doctrine is the unavailability of access to the "essential facilities"; where access exists, the doctrine serves no purpose. Thus, it is said that "essential facility claims should . . . be denied where a state or federal agency has effective power to compel sharing and to regulate its scope and terms." P. Areeda & H. Hovenkamp, Antitrust Law, p. 150, ¶773e (2003 Supp,). Respondent believes that the

---

[51] Respondent also relies upon *United States* v. *Terminal Railroad Assn. of St. Louis,* 224 U.S. 383 (1912), and *Associated Press* v. *United States,* 326 U.S. 1 (1945). These cases involved *concerted* action, which presents greater anticompetitive concerns and is amenable to a remedy that does not require judicial estimation of free-market forces: simply requiring that the outsider be granted nondiscriminatory admission to the club.

existence of sharing duties under the 1996 Act supports its case. We think the opposite: The 1996 Act's extensive provision for access makes it unnecessary to impose a judicial doctrine of forced access. To the extent respondent's "essential facilities" argument is distinct from its general §2 argument, we reject it.

IV

Finally, we do not believe that traditional antitrust principles justify adding the present case to the few existing exceptions from the proposition that there is no duty to aid competitors. Antitrust analysis must always be attuned to the particular structure and circumstances of the industry at issue. Part of that attention to economic context is an awareness of the significance of regulation. As we have noted, "careful account must be taken of the pervasive federal and state regulation characteristic of the industry." *United States* v. *Citizens & Southern Nat. Bank,* 422 U.S. 86, 91(1975); see also IA P. Areeda & H. Hovenkamp, Antitrust Law, p. 12, §240c3 (2d ed. 2000). "[A]ntitrust analysis must sensitively recognize and reflect the distinctive economic and legal setting of the regulated industry to which it applies." *Concord* v. *Boston Edison Co.,* 915 F. 2d 17, 22 (CA1 1990) (Breyer, C. J.) (internal quotation marks omitted).

One factor of particular importance is the existence of a regulatory structure designed to deter and remedy anticompetitive harm. Where such a structure exists, the additional benefit to competition provided by antitrust enforcement will tend to be small, and it will be less plausible that the antitrust laws contemplate such additional scrutiny. Where, by contrast, "[t]here is nothing built into the regulatory scheme which performs the antitrust function," *Silver* v. *New York Stock Exchange,* 373 U.S. 341, 358 (1963), the benefits of antitrust are worth its sometimes considerable disadvantages. Just as regulatory context may in other cases serve as a basis for implied immunity, see, *e.g., United States* v. *National Assn. of Securities Dealers, Inc.,* 422 U.S., at 730-735, it may also be a consideration in deciding whether to recognize an expansion of the contours of §2.

The regulatory framework that exists in this case demonstrates how, in certain circumstances, "regulation significantly diminishes the likelihood of major antitrust harm." *Concord* v. *Boston Edison Co., supra,* at 25. Consider, for example, the statutory restrictions upon Verizon's entry into the potentially lucrative market for long-distance service. To be allowed to enter the long-distance market in the first place, an incumbent LEC must be on good behavior in its local market. Authorization by the FCC requires state-by-state satisfaction of §271's competitive checklist, which as we have noted includes the non-discriminatory provision of access to UNEs. Section 271 applications to provide long-distance service have now been approved for incumbent LECs in 47 States and the District of Columbia. See FCC Authorizes SBC to Provide Long Distance Service in Illinois, Indiana, Ohio and Wisconsin (Oct. 15, 2003), http://hraunfoss.fcc.gov/edocs_public/attachmatch/DOC-239978Al.pdf.

The FCC's §271 authorization order for Verizon to provide long-distance service in New York discussed at great length Verizon's commitments to provide access to UNEs, including the provision of OSS. *In re Application by Bell Atlantic New York for Authorization Under Section 271 of the Communications Act To Provide In-Region, InterLATA Service in the State of New York,* 15 FCC Rcd. 3953, 3989-4077, ¶¶82-228 (1999) (Memorandum Opinion and Order) (hereinafter *In re Application).* Those commitments are enforceable by the FCC through continuing oversight; a failure to meet an authorization condition can result in an order that the deficiency be corrected, in the imposition of penalties, or in the suspension or revocation of long-distance approval. See 47 U.S.C. §271(d)(6)(A). Verizon also subjected itself to oversight by the PSC under a so-called "Performance Assurance Plan" (PAP). See *In re New York Telephone Co.,* 197 P.U.R. 4th 266, 280-281 (N.Y. PSC, 1999) (Order Adopting the Amended PAP) (hereinafter PAP Order). The PAP, which by its terms became binding upon FCC approval, provides specific financial penalties in the event of Verizon's failure to achieve detailed performance requirements. The FCC described Verizon's having entered into a PAP as a significant factor in its §271 authorization, because that provided "a strong financial incentive for post-entry compliance with the section 271 checklist," and prevented "backsliding." *In re Application* 3958-3959, ¶¶8, 12.

The regulatory response to the OSS failure complained of in respondent's suit provides a vivid example of how the regulatory regime operates. When several competitive LECs complained about deficiencies in Verizon's servicing of orders, the FCC and PSC responded. The FCC soon concluded that Verizon was in breach of its sharing duties under §251(c), imposed a substantial fine, and set up sophisticated measurements to gauge remediation, with weekly reporting requirements and specific penalties for failure. The PSC found Verizon in violation of the PAP even earlier, and imposed additional financial penalties and measurements with *daily* reporting requirements. In short, the regime was an effective steward of the antitrust function.

Against the slight benefits of antitrust intervention here, we must weigh a realistic assessment of its costs. Under the best of circumstances, applying the requirements of §2 "can be difficult" because "the means of illicit exclusion, like the means of legitimate competition, are myriad." *United States* v. *Microsoft Corp.,* 253 F. 3d 34, 58 (CADC 2001) (en banc) *(per curiam).* Mistaken inferences and the resulting false condemnations "are especially costly, because they chill the very conduct the antitrust laws are designed to protect." *Matsushita Elec. Industrial Co.* v. *Zenith Radio Corp.,* 475 U.S. 574, 594 (1986). The cost of false positives counsels against an undue expansion of §2 liability. One false-positive risk is that an incumbent LEC's failure to provide a service with sufficient alacrity might have nothing to do with exclusion. Allegations of violations of §251(c)(3) duties are difficult for antitrust courts to evaluate, not only because they are highly technical, but, also because they are likely to be extremely numerous, given the incessant, complex, and constantly changing interaction of competitive and incumbent LECs implementing the sharing and interconnection obligations. *Amici* States have filed a brief asserting that competitive LECs are threatened with "death by a thousand cuts." Brief for New York et al. as *Amici Curiae* 10 (internal quotation marks omitted) - the identification of which would surely be a daunting task for a generalist antitrust court. Judicial oversight under the Sherman Act would seem destined to distort investment and lead to a new layer of interminable litigation, atop the variety of litigation routes already available to and actively pursued by competitive LECs.

Even if the problem of false positives did not exist, conduct consisting of anticompetitive violations of §251 may be, as we have

32

concluded with respect to above-cost predatory pricing schemes, "beyond the practical ability of a judicial tribunal to control." *Brooke Group Ltd.* v. *Brown & Williamson Tobacco Corp.,* 509 U.S. 209, 223 (1993). Effective remediation of violations of regulatory sharing requirements will ordinarily require continuing supervision of a highly detailed decree. We think that Professor Areeda got it exactly right: "No court should impose a duty to deal that it cannot explain or adequately and reasonably supervise. The problem should be deemed irremedia[ble] by antitrust law when compulsory access requires the court to assume the day-to-day controls characteristic of a regulatory agency." Areeda, 58 Antitrust L.J., at 853. In this case, respondent has requested an equitable decree to "[p]reliminarily and permanently enjoi[n} [Verizon] from providing access to the local loop market ... to [rivals} on terms and conditions that are not as favorable" as those that Verizon enjoys. App. 49-50. An antitrust court is unlikely to be an effective day-to-day enforcer of these detailed sharing obligations.[52]

The 1996 Act is in an important respect much more ambitious than the antitrust laws. It attempts *"to eliminate the monopolies enjoyed by the inheritors of AT&T's local franchises."* *Verizon Communications Inc.* v. *FCC,* 535 U.S., at 476 (emphasis added). Section 2 of the Sherman Act, by contrast, seeks merely to prevent *unlawful monopolization.* It would be a serious mistake to conflate the two goals. The Sherman Act is indeed the "Magna Carta of free enterprise," *United States* v. *Topco Associates, Inc.,* 405 U.S. 596, 610 (1972), but it does not give judges *carte blanche* to insist that a monopolist alter its way of doing business whenever some other

---

[52] The Court of Appeals also thought that respondent's complaint might state a claim under a 'monopoly leveraging' theory (a theory barely discussed by respondent, see Brief for Respondent 24, n. 10). We disagree. To the extent the Court of Appeals dispensed with a requirement that there be a "dangerous probability of success" in monopolizing a second market, it erred, *Spectrum Sports, Inc.* v. *McQuillan,* 506 U.S. 447, 459 (1993). In any event, leveraging presupposes anticompetitive conduct, which in this case could only be the refusal-to-deal claim we have rejected.

33

approach might yield greater competition. We conclude that respondent's complaint fails to state a claim under the Sherman Act.[53]

Accordingly, the judgment of the Court of Appeals is reversed, and the case is remanded for further proceedings consistent with this opinion.

---

[53] Our disposition makes it unnecessary to consider petitioner's alternative contention that respondent lacks antitrust standing. See *Steel Co.* v. *Citizens for Better Environment,* 523 U.S. 83, 97, and n. 2 (1998); *National Railroad Passenger Corporation* v. *National Assn. of Railroad Passengers,* 414 U.S. 453, 456 (1974).

Insert following Note 3 at page 812

Note on the EU *Microsoft* decision

In 2004, the European Commission (the executive arm of the European Union) issued a far-reaching decision against Microsoft, finding that the software company violated European competition rules by abusing its dominant position in the market for personal computer operating systems (OS). *Sun Microsystems* v. *Microsoft Corp.*, EC Comm 1 (Comp/C-3/37.792) (March 24, 2004) ("European Commission Decision"), *online at* http://europa.eu.int/comm/competition/antitrust/cases/decisions/37792/en.pdf (visited July 19, 2005). Specifically, the Commission found that Microsoft illegally leveraged its dominant position in the OS market into two adjacent markets: (1) the market for work group server (WGS) operating systems, and (2) the market for media players.

In the server market, Microsoft had refused to disclose documentation that would allow its competitors to create server software that is fully compatible with PCs that use the popular Microsoft Windows OS. The Commission held that this nondisclosure put competitors at an unfair disadvantage and risked eliminating competition in the WGS market. It held that Microsoft's actions created a significant risk of eliminating competition in the WGS market and that this violated Article 82(b) of the EU Treaty, which forbids a company from abusing its dominant position by "limiting production, markets or technical development to the prejudice of consumers." Treaty Establishing the European Community ("EC Treaty"), Common Rules on Competition, Taxation and Approximation of Laws, Art. 82 (1958). The Commission ordered Microsoft to disclose the relevant information within 120 days of the decision, but it allowed Microsoft to receive reasonable compensation to the extent that the information being disclosed was entitled to protection as intellectual property.

The Commission also found that Microsoft abused its dominant position by tying its Windows Media Player (WMP) with the Windows OS, a charge similar to the one the company faced in the

35

United States relating to its web browser software. By bundling its media software with Windows, Microsoft unfairly placed its competitors in that market at a competitive disadvantage and reduced consumer choice in violation of Article 82. The Commission ordered Microsoft to offer a version of the Windows OS without the WMP to its customers within 90 days of its decision.

The Commission concluded that Microsoft's violations were severe enough to warrant drastic penalties:

Microsoft's anti-competitive behaviour weakens effective competition on the markets for work group server operating systems and media players in an appreciable way. Microsoft's refusal to supply interface information brings about a risk of elimination of competition on the world-wide market for work group server operating systems. Microsoft's tying of WMP with Windows risks impairing the effective structure of competition in the world-wide market for media players. European Commission Decision at para. 992.

In addition to enjoining Microsoft from continuing its abusive activity, the Commission levied a record fine of over €497 million (about $603 million) in the hopes of deterring Microsoft or others from engaging in similar conduct.

This decision went considerably further than the consent decree that was ultimately entered between the United States and Microsoft in the corresponding U.S. litigation. See *United States v. Microsoft Corp.,* 2002-2 Trade Cas. (CCH) ¶ 73,860, 2002 WL 31654530 (D.D.C. Nov. 12, 2002), which imposes certain conduct restrictions on Microsoft, but does not require Microsoft to issue two different versions of its operating system. Although it is possible that part of the difference is attributable to the fact that the U.S. decree was entered by consent and the EU decision was not, query whether the real difference is between the cautious approach toward tying arrangements reflected in the D.C. Circuit's opinion, casebook at 765, and the more aggressive approach used by the Commission.

Replace note 9, page 873, with the following:

UNITED STATES v. AMR CORP., AMERICAN AIRLINES INC.

United States Court of Appeals, Tenth Circuit, 2003, 335 F.3d 1109

Before J. LUCERO, PORFILIO, AND MURPHY, Circuit Judges.

LUCERO, J. This case involves the nature of permissible competitive practices in the airline industry under the antitrust laws of this country, centered around the hub-and-spoke system of American Airlines. The United States brought this suit against AMR Corporation, American Airlines, Inc., and American Eagle Holding Corporation ("American'), alleging monopolization and attempted monopolization through predatory pricing in violation of § 2 of the Sherman Act. In essence, the government alleges that American engaged in multiple episodes of price predation in four city-pair airline markets, all connected to American's hub at Dallas/Fort Worth International Airport ("DFW"), with the ultimate purpose of using the reputation for predatory pricing it earned in those four markets to defend a monopoly at its DFW hub. At its root, the government's complaint alleges that American: (1) priced its product on the routes in question below cost; and (2) intended to recoup these losses by charging supracompetitive prices either on the four core routes themselves, or on those routes where it stands to exclude competition by means of its "reputation for predation." Finding that the government failed to demonstrate the existence of a genuine issue of material fact as to either of these allegations, the district court granted summary judgment in favor of American, from which the government now appeals. Because we agree that the record is void of evidence that rises to the level of a material conflict, we affirm.

I

Airlines are predominantly organized in a hub-and-spoke system, with traffic routed such that passengers leave their origin city for an intermediate hub airport. Passengers traveling to a concentrated hub tend of pay higher average fares than those traveling

37

on comparable routes that do not include a concentrated hub as an endpoint. This is known as the "hub premium" and a major airline's hub is often an important profit center. Entry of low cost carriers ("LCCs") into a hub market tends to drive down the fares charged by major carriers. Consequently, major carriers generally enjoy higher margins on routes where they do not face LCC competition.

Both American and Delta Airlines ("Delta") maintain hubs at DFW, though Delta's presence is considerably smaller than American's. As of May 2000, American's share of passengers boarded at DFW was 70.2%, Delta's share was roughly 18%, and LCC share was 2.4%. As of mid-2000, there were seven low-cost airlines serving DFW. In the period between 1997 to 2000, five new low-cost airlines entered DFW: American, Trans Air, Frontier, National, Sun Country, and Ozark. DFW has more low-fare airlines than any other hub airport and the number of passengers carried by low-fare airlines increased by over 30% from May 1999 to May 2000. Nevertheless, LCCs have a significantly higher market share in some other major U.S. hubs.

LCCs generally enjoy the advantage of having lower costs than major carriers, allowing them to offer lower fares than their major-airline competitors. During the period between 1995 and 1997, a number of LCCs, including Vanguard, Western Pacific, and Sunjet, began to take advantage of these lower costs of entering certain city-pair routes serving DFW and charging lower fares than American. The instant case primarily involves DFW-Kansas City, DFW-Wichita, DFW-Colorado Springs, and DFW-Long Beach.

American responded to lower LCC fares on these routes with changes in: (1) pricing (matching LCC prices); (2) capacity (adding flights or switching to larger planes); and (3) yield management (making more seats available at the new, lower prices). By increasing capacity, American overrode its own internal capacity-planning models for each route, which had previously indicated that such increases would be unprofitable. In each instance, American's response produced the same result: the competing LCC failed to establish a presence, moved its operations, American generally resumed its prior marketing strategy, reducing flights and raising prices to levels roughly comparable to those prior to the period of low-fare competition. Capacity was reduced after LCC exit, but usually remained higher than prior to the alleged episode of predatory activity.

The government filed suit on May 13, 1999, alleging that American participated in a scheme of predatory pricing in violation of § 2 of the Sherman Act. In the government's view, American's combined response of lowering prices, increasing capacity, and altering yield management in response to LCC competition constituted an unlawful, anticompetitive response. After reviewing a voluminous record and receiving extensive briefs, the district court granted American's motion for summary judgment on all antitrust claims, concluding that the government failed to demonstrate the existence of a genuine issue of material fact as to (1) whether American had priced below costs and (2) whether American had a dangerous probability of recouping its alleged investment in below-cost prices.

. . . Monopolization claims under § 2 of the Sherman Act require proof: (1) that a firm has monopoly power in a properly defined relevant market; and (2) that it willfully acquired or maintained this power by means of anticompetitive conduct. *TV Communications Network, Inc.* v. *Turner Network Television, Inc.,* 964 F.2d 1022, 1025 (10th Cir. 1992). This is to be distinguished from a business that acquired monopoly power by greater skill, efficiency, or by "building a better mousetrap." Claims of attempted monopolization under § 2 of the Sherman Act require four elements of proof: (1) a relevant geographic and product market; (2) specific intent to monopoize the market; (3) anticompetitive conduct in furtherance of the attempt; and (4) a dangerous probability that the firm will succeed in the attempt. *Multistate Legal Studies, Inc.* v. *Harcourt Brace Jovanovich Legal and Prof'l Publ'ns, Inc.,* 63 F.3d 1540, 1550 (10th Cir. 1995).

In the instant case, the anticompetitive conduct at issue is predatory pricing. The crux of the government's argument is that the "incremental" revenues and costs specifically associated with American" capacity additions show a loss. Because American spent more to add capacity than the revenues generated by the capacity additions, such capacity additions made no economic sense unless

American intended to drive LCCs out of the market. Under the government'' theory, American attempted to monopolize the four city-pair routes in question in order to develop a reputation as an exceedingly aggressive competitor and set an example to all potential competitors. Fearing American's predatory response, the theory goes, future potential competitors will decline to enter other DFW market routes and compete. If American succeeds in preventing or at least forestalling the formation of an LCC hub at DFW, it will then be able to charge higher prices on other DFW routes and thereby recoup the losses it incurred from its "capacity dumping" on the four core routes.

III

Scholars from the Chicago School of economic thought have long labeled predatory pricing as implausible and irrational. Frank Easterbrook, a leader of the Chicago School, once concluded that "there is not sufficient reason for antitrust law or the courts to take predation seriously." Frank H. Easterbrook, *Predatory Strategies & Counterstrategies*, 48 U. Chi. L. Rev. 263, 264 (1981). Chicago scholars argued that lowering prices could only be pro-competitive and any prohibition on such conduct could ultimately deter firms from engaging in conduct that is socially beneficial. Richard J. Pierce, Jr., Is Post-Chicago Ready for the Courtroom? A Response to Professor Brennan, 69 Geo. Wash. L. Rev. 1103, 1106 (2001). Commentators viewed below-cost pricing as irrational largely because of the uncertainty of recouping losses through later price increases. In order for a predatory pricing scheme to be successful, two future events had to take place: first, the victim of the alleged predation would have to exist and, second, the predator would have to generate profits in excess of its initial losses. Jonathan B. Baker, Predatory Pricing after Brooke Group: An Economic Perspective, 62 Antitrust L.J. 585, 586 (1994). In two seminal antitrust opinions, the Supreme Court adopted the skepticism of Chicago scholars, observing that "there is a consensus among commentators that predatory pricing schemes are rarely tried, and even more rarely successful." *Matsushita Elec. Indus. Co.* v. *Zenith Radio Corp.*, 475 U.S. 574, 489, 106 S.Ct. 1348, 89 L.Ed.2d 528 (1986); *Brooke Group Ltd.* v. *Brown & Williamson Tobacco Corp.*, 509 U.S. 209, 226, 113 S.Ct. 2578, 125 L.Ed.2d 168 (1993). Implausibility of predatory pricing schemes was said to flow from the fact that their success is inherently uncertain. *Matsushita,*

475 U.S. at 598, 106 S.Ct. 1348. While "the short-run loss is definite . . . the long-run gain depends on successfully neutralizing the competition. *Id.* Moreover, "[t]he success of any predatory scheme depends on *maintaining* monopoly power for long enough both to recoup the pedator's losses and to harvest some additional gain." *Id.* Furthermore, caution in predatory pricing cases is the watchword as "the costs of an erroneous finding are high." *Brooke Group*, 509 U.S. at 227, 113 S.Ct. 2578. Because "the mechanism by which a firm engages in predatory pricing – lowering prices – is the same mechanism by which a firm stimulates competition," mistaken inferences may deter the very conduct the antitrust laws were created to protect. *Cargill Inc.* v. *Monfort of Colo.*, 479 U.S. 104, 122, 107 S.Ct. 484, 93 L.Ed.2d 427 (1986). Recent scholarship has challenged the notion that predatory pricing schemes are implausible and irrational. *See, e.g.*, Patrick Bolton et al., <u>Predatory Pricing: Strategic Theory and Legal Policy</u>, 88 Geo. L.J. 2239, 2241 (2000) ("Modern economic analysis has developed coherent theories of predation that contravene earlier economic writing claiming that predatory pricing conduct is irrational.") Post-Chicago economists have theorized that price predation is not only plausible, but profitable, especially in a multi-market coontext where predation can occur in one market and recoupment can occur rapidly in other markets. *See* Baker, *supra*, at 590.

Although this court approaches the matter with caution, we do not do so with the incredulity that once prevailed.

IV

The Supreme Court has formulated two prerequisites to recovery on a predatory pricing claim, conditions that "are not easy to establish." *Brook Group*, 509 U.S. at 227, 113 S.Ct. 2578. First, the government must prove that "the prices complained of are below an appropriate measure of [American's] costs." *Id.* at 223, 113 S.Ct. 2578. While the first element is crucial, "[t]hat below-cost pricing may impose painful losses on its target is of no moment to the antitrust laws if competition is not injured." *Id.* at 225, 113 S.Ct. 2578. Thus, the second prerequisite to recovery on a predatory pricing claim, a demonstration that American had "a dangerous probability of recouping its investment in below-cost prices," must

41

also be met. *Id.* at 224, 113 S.Ct. 2578. Without a dangerous probability of recoupment, competition remains unharmed even if individual competitors suffer. As frequently notes, "the antitrust laws were passed for the protection of *competition*, not *competitors.*" *Id.* (citing *Brown Shoe Co.* v. *United States*, 370 U.S. 294, 320, 82 S.Ct. 1502, 8 L.Ed.2d 510 (1962)).

Speaking to the first prerequisite to recovery, the Supreme Court stated that "[p]redatory pricing means pricing below some appropriate measure of cost." *Matsushita*, 475 U.S. at 584 n. 8, 106 S.Ct. 1348.[54] Despite a great deal of debate on the subject, no consensus has emerged as to what the most "appropriate" measure of cost is in predatory pricing cases. Costs can generally be divided into those that are "fixed" and do not vary with the level of output (management expenses, interest on bonded debt, property taxes, deprecation, and other irreducible overhead) and those that are "variable" and do vary with the level of output (materials, fuel, labor used to produce the product). Marginal cost, the cost that results from producing an additional increment of output, is primarily a function of variable cost because fixed costs, as the name would imply, are largely unaffected by changes in output. *See Rebel Oil Co., Inc.* v. *Atl. Richfield Co.*, 146 F.3d 1088, 1092 (9th Cir. 1998). For predatory pricing cases, especially those involving allegedly predatory production increases, the ideal measure of cost would be marginal cost because "[a]s long as a firm's prices exceed its marginal cost, each additional sale decreases losses or increases profits." *Advo*, 51

---

[54] The government notes in its brief that the "gravamen of the complaint is not limited to American's pricing." Rather, the complained of behavior includes American's capacity additions. However, as the district court correctly noted, prices and productive output are "two sides of the same coin." *United States* v. *AMR Corp.*, 140 F.Supp. 2d 1141, 1194 (D. Kan. 2001). While the specific behavior complained of in the instant case is an increase in output or frequency, these actions must be analyzed in terms of their effect on price and cost. Thus, in order to succeed in the present action, the government must meet the standards of proof for predatory pricing cases established in *Brooke Group*.

F.3d at 1198. However, marginal cost, an economic abstraction, is notoriously difficult to measure and "cannot be determined from conventional accounting methods." *Northeastern Tel. Co. v. AT&T*, 651 F.2d 76, 88 (2nd Cir. 1981); *Pac. Eng'g & Prod. Co. of Nev. v. Kerr-McGee Corp.*, 551 F.2d 790, 797 (10th Cir. 1977). Economists, therefore, must resort to proxies for marginal cost. A commonly accepted proxy for marginal cost in predatory pricing cases in Average Variable Cost ("AVC"), the average of those costs that vary with the level of output. *See, e.g., Stearns Airport Equip. Co. v. FMC Corp.*, 170 F.3d 518, 532 (5th Cir. 1999); *Advo*, 51 F.3d at 1198; *Arthur S. Langenderfer, Inc. v. S.E. Johnson Co.*, 729 F.2d 1050, 1056 (6th Cir. 1984); *Northeastern Tel.*, 651 F.2d at 88.

The Supreme Court has declined to state which of the various cost measures is definitive. In *Brooke Group*, the Court accepted for the purposes of the case the parties' agreement that the appropriate measure of cost was AVC, but declined to "resolve the conflict among the lower courts over the appropriate measure of cost." 509 U.S. at 223 n. 1, 113 S.Ct. 2578. In this circuit, we have spoken of both AVC and other marginal cost measures as relevant. *See, e.g., Multistate Legal Studies*, 63 F.3d at 1549 n. 5 (observing that "evidence of marginal cost or average variable cost is extremely beneficial in establishing a case of monopoization through predatory pricing" (emphasis added)); *Pac. Eng'g*, 551 F.2d at 797. Because there may be times when courts need the flexibility to examine both AVC as well as other proxies for marginal cost in order to evaluate an alleged predatory pricing scheme, we again decline to dictate a definitive cost measure for all cases. Sole reliance on AVC as the appropriate measure of cost may obscure the nature of a particular predatory scheme and, thus, contrary to what is suggested by the district court, we do not favor AVC to the exclusion of other proxies for marginal cost. Whatever the proxy used to measure marginal cost, it must be accurate and reliable in the specific circumstances of the case at bar.

Conceding that AVC is a good proxy for marginal cost in most cases, the government nevertheless argues that there may be times when looking only to a market-wide AVC test will disguise the nature of the predatory conduct at issue. Where there is a challenge to well-defined incremental conduct, and where incremental costs may be directly and confidently measured utilizing alternative proxies to AVC, argues the government, the market-wide AVC test is inappropriate.

Considering this to be the situation in the instant case, the government proffers four tests that purport to measure reliably incremental costs – the price costs associated with the capacity additions at issue. Rather than creating independent measures of the costs associated with American's capacity additions, the government's experts rely on cost measures used in AAIMSPAN, American's internal decisional accounting system (accounting measures that are used for internal decision making, not financial reporting). The government notes that a range of tests are necessary to rule out false positives and avoid misleading indications of predation. Due to similarities among the four tests, the district court grouped them as Tests Two and Three, and Tests One and Four for purposes of analysis. We proceed to consider each test to determine whether it is valid as a matter of law.

Two of the tests grouped together by the district court, Tests Two and Three, purport to measure incremental costs by looking to whether certain of American's internal cost-accounting measures became negative following the allegedly predatory capacity additions. Both tests rely on an internal accounting measure known as FAUDNC, or "Fully Allocated earnings plus Upline/Downline contribution Net of Costs." *United States* v. *AMR Corp.*, 140 F.Supp. 2d 1141, 1175 (D. Kan. 2001). As the name would imply, FAUDNC is a fully allocated earnings measure, meaning that general operating expenses are arbitrarily allocated by American's decision accounting system to the flight or route level, and do not necessarily represent the exact costs associated with a particular flight or route. FAUDNC reflects 97-99% of American's total costs, which include fixed costs not affected by the capacity additions at issue. Thus, while FAUDNC includes some costs directly caused by a particular flight or operations on a particular route (such as fuel and landing fees), it also includes many costs that are not related to the operation of a particular flight or route (dispatch, city ticket offices, certain station expenses, certain maintenance expenses, American's flight academy, flight simulator maintenance, general sales and advertising). In other words,

FAUDNC includes costs that are not entirely avoidable even if American were to abandon an entire route.

Because Tests Two and Three rely on fully allocated costs and include many fixed costs, the district court held that utilizing these cost measures would be the equivalent of applying an average total cost test, implicitly ruled out by *Brooke Group*'s mention of incremental costs only.[55] The district court therefore concluded that, by relying on FAUDNC, Tests Two and Three were, by definition, not measures of marginal or incremental cost. We agree with this conclusion. While we will accept alternative proxies to marginal cost beyond AVC, Tests Two and Three are simply not proxies for marginal or incremental cost. Moreover, because these tests rely on "arbitrary allocation of costs among different classes of service," they "cannot purport to identify those costs which are *caused* by a product or service, and this is fundamental to economic cost determination." *MCI Communications Corp.* v. *AT&T,* 708 F.2d 1081, 1116 (7th Cir. 1982). Thus, given that Tests Two and Three rely on cost measures that are not, in large part, variable or avoidable with respect to capacity increases, we conclude that they are invalid as a matter of law as a measure of allegedly predatory capacity increases.[56] *See*

---

[55] While the government has not completely abandoned Tests Two and Three on appeal, it has not chosen to press them beyond a statement in a footnote of their Reply Brief noting that "American's criticisms of Tests 2 and 3 are incorrect." (Appellant's Reply Br. at 12). Notably, the government has previously taken the position that utilizing fully allocated costs as a pricing standard would result in "stultification of competition" and should be rejected as "contrary to the public interest." *S. Pac. Communications Co.* v. *AT&T,* 556 F.Supp. 825, 923 n. 107 (D.D.C. 1982).

[56] In holding that Tests Two and Three are invalid as a matter of law, we consider the uncontested fact that these tests, by relying on FAUDNC, measure a significant amount of American's fixed costs. As such, Tests Two and Three are inappropriate measures of incremental costs under *Brooke Group*, as they cannot demonstrate that American priced below an "appropriate measure of cost" with respect to the challenged capacity additions.

Stearns, 170 F.3d at 532 (noting that "judgment as a matter of law is appropriate when a plaintiff fails to adequately specify how the challenged pricing undercuts the defendant's variable costs").

As to Tests One and Four, the district court grouped them together, labeling them as short-run profit-maximization tests. Test One examines changes in profitability. It employs FAUDNC, discussed above, and an internal measure of American's variable costs known as VAUDNC, as well as a version of VAUDNC that has been modified by the government, VAUDNC-AC.[57] If these measures declined following a capacity addition, this test allegedly demonstrates that adding capacity forced American to forgo better profit performance elsewhere. Test Four relies on VAUDNC-AC to compare the supposed revenue from incremental passengers with the average avoidable cost of adding capacity. Under Test Four, if incremental revenues are below incremental costs, this is "evidence of sacrifice." *AMR Corp.*, 140 F.Supp. 2d at 1180.

In rejecting Tests One and Four, the district court concluded that they were, in essence, short-run profit-maximization tests that focus on whether a company has sacrificed some level of profit to compete more effectively. Courts and scholars have observed that such a sacrifice test would necessarily involve a great deal of speculation and often result in injury to the consumer and a chilling of competition. *See* 3 Phillip E. Areeda & Herbert Hovenkamp,

---

[57] Unlike the other costs measures, which are taken straight out of American's internal accounting system, VAUDNC-AC is a government creation. It represents VAUDNC costs plus the cost of aircraft ownership, which is traditionally considered a fixed cost in the airline industry, not an avoidable cost of changes in capacity on a route. By treating aircraft ownership as a variable expense, this measure reduces the apparent performance of the routes by increasing the costs attributed to operations on a particular flight or route. VAUDNC-AC represents over 79% of the total costs in American's decision accounting system. The district court concluded that VAUDNC-AC overstates short-run cost because it includes fixed, unavoidable aircraft-ownership costs.

Antitrust Law ¶ 736c2 (2d ed. 2002); *Stearns*, 170 F.3d at 533 n. 14 (nothing that theories of predation based upon the failure to maximize profits in the short run are "no longer tenable in the wake of *Brooke Group*"). Upon closer examination, it is clear that rather than determining whether the added capacity itself was priced below an appropriate measure of cost, Test One effectively treats forgone or "sacrificed" profits as costs, and condemns activity that may have been profitable as predatory.[58] Rather than isolating the costs actually associated with the capacity additions the government purports to measure directly, Test One simply performs a "before-and-after" comparison of the route as a whole, looking to whether profits on the route as a whole decline after capacity was added, not to whether the challenged capacity additions were done below cost. In the end, Test One indicates only that a company has failed to maximize short-run profits on the route as a whole. Such a pricing standard could lead to a strangling of competition, as it would condemn nearly all output expansions, and harm to consumers. We conclude that Test One is

---

[58]   For example, if an airline earned $20.6 million on a route that cost $18 million to operate, it would have $2.6 million in profit. If the airline then added a flight to the route that would cost $500,000 to operate, but brought in an additional $1 million in revenue from passengers, the airline would make $500,000 profit. If adding this extra capacity to the route reduced the profitability of other flights on that route, reducing revenue for the rest of the route by $600,000 down to $20 million, under Test One, this conduct would be considered predatory because rather than comparing the additional flight's $1 million in revenue to its $500,000 in costs, Test One looks only to the reduction in profits on the route as a whole from $2.6 million to $2.5 million. Thus, this conduct would be labeled predatory because the profits for the route as a whole declined, even though the capacity additions themselves were profitable and the route as a whole was still profitable. *See* Einer Elhauge, "Why Above-Cost Price Cuts to Drive Out Entrants are Not Predatory – and the Implications for Defining Costs and Market Power," 112 Yale L.J. 681, 694 (2003). It is clear, therefore, that, in proffering Test One, the government has not "attempted to identify the actual costs associated with the capacity additions." *AMR Corp.*, 140 F.Supp. 2d at 1202.

invalid as a matter of law. Test Four does not appear to suffer from this flaw, and we do not reject it for being a short-run profit-maximization test.

As with Test One, the district court noted that, in proffering Test Four, the government has not "identif[ied] the actual costs associated with the capacity additions." *AMR Corp.*, 140 F.Supp. 2d at 1202. We agree with this conclusion as well. Test Four attempts to reveal American's predatory conduct by measuring and comparing the incremental costs incurred by American when it added capacity to the city-pair routes in question to the incremental revenue it received from the additional capacity. The government's expert who developed Test Four, Steven Berry, characterized it as a comparison of the "average revenue from incremental passengers who traveled after the capacity addition with the average avoidable cost of the capacity addition" *See also* William J. Baumol, "Predation and the Logic of the Average Variable Cost Test," 39 J.L. & Econ. 49, 58 (1996) (opining that average avoidable cost is the proper cost measure for predatory pricing tests). Berry further stated that, when considering an increase in capacity, an avoidable cost test compares, "the *incremental revenue generated by the increment* of capacity to the *avoidable cost of the increment* of capacity." Therefore, the only appropriate costs included in Test Four are those costs that American could have avoided by not adding the challenged capacity to the city-pair routes. Test Four utilizes VAUDNC-AC, the cost component of which includes both aircraft ownership costs and costs characterized as variable over an eighteen-month planning period by AAIMSPAN. *See AMR Corp.*, 140 F.Supp. 2d at 1174-75. The costs included in VAUDNC-AC include variable costs American incurs with respect to all of its operations at DFW. Because some of those variable costs do not vary proportionately with the level of flight activity, they are allocated arbitrarily to a flight or route by AAIMSPAN. American identifies these variable, non-proportional common costs as: (1) airport ticket agents, (2) arrival agents, (3) ramp workers, and (4) security. Therefore, American argues that because VAUDNC-AC is an allocated variable cost measure, it cannot b used to calculate the *avoidable* cost of the added capacity.

The government first responds to American's criticism by arguing that cost allocation is a key component of managerial accounting and a relevant and sensible method by which to assign costs for decision-making purposes. While the government may be correct, this court is not presented with the question of whether cost allocation is a reasonable *accounting* method or a technique which provides businesses with reliable data to evaluate business decisions. Because the government asserts that Test Four measures average *avoidable* cost, this court must instead determine whether that assertion is correct. Thus, the government's first response is wholly irrelevant. The government also alleges that there exists a genuine issue of material fact because its expert reworked Test Four so as to omit the contested costs and the results still indicated predation. The government's expert, however, states that when he reworked the numbers in response to criticism from American's expert, he eliminated the following costs from the test: (1) CTO ticketing, (2) direct reservations, (3) reservation communications, (4) cargo reservations, (5) and dispatch. Although the propriety of including these costs in Test Four was also disputed by American, they are not the costs that American disputed on the grounds that they are allocated arbitrarily to a route of flight by AAIMSPAN. Consequently, the expert's revisions to Test Four are not responsive to American's criticism and no genuine issue of material fact exists.

Because the cost component of Test Four includes arbitrarily allocated variable costs, it does not compare incremental revenue to average avoidable cost. Instead, it compares incremental revenue to a measure of both average variable cost and average avoidable cost. Therefore, Test Four does not measure only the avoidable or incremental cost of the capacity additions and cannot be used to satisfy the government's burden in this case. We conclude that all four proxies are invalid as a matter of law, fatally flawed in their application, and fundamentally unreliable.[59] Because it is uncontested

---

[59] The government's four proxies are, in effect, an illustration of the long-recognized fact that "the true marginal costs of production are difficult to generate." *Stearns*, 170 F.3d at 532. The difficulty inherent in isolating the precise costs associated with production increases is precisely why most courts attempt to "estimate [marginal cost] by using average variable costs." *Id.*, *see also Morgan* v. *Ponder*, 892 F.2d 1355, 1362 n. 17 (noting that "where it is difficult

Footnote continued on next page

that American did not price below AVC for any route as a whole, we agree with the district court's conclusion that the government has not succeeded in establishing the first element of *Brooke Group*, pricing below an appropriate measure of cost.[60] Our conclusion that the government has not succeeded in establishing a genuine issue of material fact as to the first prong of *Brooke Group*, pricing below an appropriate measure of cost, renders an examination of whether the government has succeeded in creating a genuine issue of material fact as to the second prong of *Brooke Group*, dangerous probability of recoupment, unnecessary. Given the exceedingly thin line between vigorous price competition and predatory pricing, *see Northeastern Telephone Co.*, 651 F.2 at 88, the balance the Supreme Court has struck in *Brooke Group*, and the fatally flawed nature of the alternative pricing proxies proffered by the government, we conclude that the summary judgment in favor of American was appropriate.

Footnote continued from previous page
to isolate variable costs . . . the plaintiff should be required to prove across-the-board predatory pricing").

[60] The district court also stated that even if American had priced below an appropriate measure of cost, it was nevertheless entitled to summary judgment because "American's prices only matched, and never undercut, the fares of the new entrant, low cost carriers on the four core routes." *AMR Corp.*, 140 F.Supp. 2d at 1204. In so concluding the district court essentially imported the statutory "meeting competition" defense from the Robinson-Patman Act, 15 U.S.C. § 13(b). While we have never applied the "meeting competition" defense in a § 2 predatory pricing case, the district court reasoned that "there is strong inferential support for the idea that the defense may be appropriate in a given case." *Id.* at 1204. There may be strong arguments for application of the meeting competition defense in the Sherman Act context by analogy to the Robinson-Patman context. However, unlike in the Robinson-Patman Act, such a defense is not expressly provided for by the terms of the Sherman Act. The Supreme Court has never mentioned the possibility of such a defense under the Sherman Act. We therefore decline to rule that the "meeting competition" defense applies in the § 2 context.

The order of the district court granting summary judgment to American is AFFIRMED.

CHAPTER 8: ADDITIONAL LIMITATIONS ON A
SINGLE FIRM'

Insert after Note Cases on Tying Law, p. 886

NOTE

Independent Ink v. *Illinois Tool Works Inc.*, 396 F.3rd 1342
(Fed. Circuit 2005). Tridant, a subsidiary of Illinois Tool Works, held
a patent on print-head technology to manufacture printers, usually
used to place barcodes on cartons. Tridant also manufactured and
sold ink and its standard contract provided that it would license its
ink-printing device only if used in connection with ink supplied by
Tridant. Independent Inc., a competitor of Tridant in the ink market,
challenged the licensing arrangement as a tie-in sale under Section 1
and monopolization under Section 2.

With respect to the tie-in sale, Independent Inc. did not prove
that the patent on print-head technology conferred significant
economic power but rather relied on *International Salt* (tying the
purchase of salt to the lease of patented salt utilization machines was
a violation without inquiry into defendant's market power) and *United
States* v. *Loews*, 371 U.S. 38 (1962) concluding that when tying of
patented or copyrighted products - in Loews the tying of less popular
films to popular copyrighted films - market power can be presumed
where the tying product is patented or copyrighted.

Plaintiffs argued that the concurring opinion in *Jefferson
Parish* is now the law and concluded that *International Salt* and
Loews were no longer good law, and also cited numerous academic
articles criticizing Supreme Court cases relying on a presumption of
market power in patent and copyright cases. *See, e.g.*, Areeda,
Elhauge and Hovenkamp, 10 Antitrust Law § 1737c (2nd Ed 2004),
Posner, Antitrust Law 197-98 (2nd Ed 2001). The Federal Circuit
refused to reverse on the basis of an ambiguous concurring opinion
and extensive academic criticism:

"... The Court's 'decisions remain binding precedent until [it] see[s] fit to reconsider them, regardless of whether subsequent cases have raised doubts about their continuing vitality.... If a precedent of th[e] Court has direct application in a case, yet appears to rest on reasons rejected in some other line of decisions, the Court of Appeals should follow the case which directly controls, leaving to the Court the prerogative of overruling its own decisions."

The Supreme Court has granted certiorari and the *Independent Ink* case is scheduled for review before the Supreme Court in the 2005-2006 term of the Court.

Insert at the end of Note 2, page 961.

UNITED STATES v. DENTSPLY INTERNATIONAL, INC.

United States Court of Appeals, Third Circuit, 2005

399 F.3d 181

Before McKEE, ROSENN J. WEIS, Circuit Judges

WEIS, J. In this antitrust case we conclude that an exclusivity policy imposed by a manufacturer on its dealers violates Section 2 of the Sherman Act. We come to that position because of the nature of the relevant market and the established effectiveness of the restraint despite the lack of long term contracts between the manufacturer and its dealers. Accordingly, we will reverse the judgment of the District Court in favor of the defendant and remand with directions to grant the Government's request for injunctive relief.

The Government alleged that Defendant, Dentsply International, Inc., acted unlawfully to maintain a monopoly in violation of Section 2 of the Sherman Act, 15 U.S.C. § 2; entered into illegal restrictive dealing agreements prohibited by Section 3 of the Clayton Act, 15 U.S.C. § 14; and used unlawful agreements in restraint of interstate trade in violation of Section 1 of the Sherman Act, 15 U.S.C. § 1. After a bench trial, the District Court denied the injunctive relief sought by the Government and entered judgment for defendant.

In its comprehensive opinion, the District Court found the following facts. Dentsply International, Inc. is a Delaware Corporation with its principal place of business in York Pennsylvania. It manufactures artificial teeth for use in dentures and other restorative appliances and sells them to dental products dealers. The dealers, in turn, supply the teeth and various other materials to dental laboratories, which fabricate dentures for sale to dentists.

The relevant market is the sale of prefabricated artificial teeth in the United States.

Because of advances in dental medicine, artificial tooth manufacturing is marked by a low or no-growth potential. Dentsply has long dominated the industry consisting of 12-13 manufacturers and enjoys a 75%--80% market share on a revenue basis, 67% on a unit basis, and is about 15 times larger than its next closest competitor. The other significant manufacturers and their market shares are:

5%	Ivoclar Vivadent, Inc.
3%	Vita Zahnfabrik
3%	[61] Myerson LLC
2%	[61] American Tooth Industries
1%-2%	[61] Universal Dental Company
1%	Heraeus Kulzer GmbH
1%	Davis, Schottlander & Davis, Ltd.

Dealers sell to dental laboratories a full range of metals, porcelains, acrylics, waxes, and other materials required to fabricate fixed or removal restorations. Dealers maintain large inventories of artificial teeth and carry thousands of products, other than teeth, made by hundreds of different manufacturers. Dentsply supplies $400 million of products other than teeth to its network of 23 dealers.

There are hundreds of dealers who compete on the basis of price and service among themselves, as well as with manufacturers who sell directly to laboratories. The dealer field has experienced significant consolidation with several large national and regional firms emerging.

For more than fifteen years, Dentsply has operated under a policy that discouraged its dealers from adding competitors' teeth to their lines of products. In 1993, Dentsply adopted "Dealer Criterion 6." It provides that in order to effectively promote Dentsply-York products, authorized dealers "may not add further tooth lines to their product offering." Dentsply operates on a purchase order basis with

---

[61]   These companies sell directly to dental laboratories as well as to dealers.

its distributors and, therefore, the relationship is essentially terminable at will. Dealer Criterion 6 was enforced against dealers with the exception of those who had carried competing products before 1993 and were "grandfathered" for sales of those products. Dentsply rebuffed attempts by those particular distributors to expand their lines of competing products beyond the grandfathered ones.

Dentsply's five top dealers sell competing grandfathered brands of teeth. In 2001, their share of Dentsply's overall sales were

Zahn	39%
Patterson	28%
Darby	8%
Benco	4%
DLDS	<4%

TOTAL....	83%

16,000 dental laboratories fabricate restorations and a subset of 7,000 provide dentures. The laboratories compete with each other on the basis of price and service. Patients and dentists value fast service, particularly in the case of lost or damaged dentures. When laboratories' inventories cannot supply the necessary teeth, dealers may fill orders for walk-ins or use over-night express mail as does Dentsply, which dropped-shipped some 60% of orders from dealers.

Dealers have been dissatisfied with Dealer Criterion 6, but, at least in the recent past, none of them have given up the popular Dentsply teeth to take on a competitive line. Dentsply at one time considered selling directly to the laboratories, but abandoned the concept because of fear that dealers would retaliate by refusing to buy its other dental products.

In the 1990's Dentsply implemented aggressive sales campaigns, including efforts to promote its teeth in dental schools, providing rebates for laboratories' increased usage, and deploying a sales force dedicated to teeth, rather than the entire product mix. Its chief competitors did not as actively promote their products. Foreign manufacturers were slow to alter their designs to cope with American preferences, and, in at least one instance, pursued sales of porcelain products rather than plastic teeth.

Dentsply has had a reputation for aggressive price increases in the market and has created a high price umbrella. Its artificial tooth business is characterized as a "cash cow" whose profits are diverted to other operations of the company. A report in 1996 stated its profits from teeth since 1990 had increased 32% from $16.8 million to $22.2 million.

The District Court found that Dentsply's business justification for Dealer Criterion 6 was pretextual and designed expressly to exclude its rivals from access to dealers. The Court however concluded that other dealers were available and direct sales to laboratories was a viable method of doing business. Moreover, it concluded that Dentsply had not created a market with supra competitive pricing, dealers were free to leave the network at any time, and the Government failed to prove that Dentsply's actions "have been or could be successful in preventing 'new or potential competitors from gaining a foothold in the market.'" *United States v. Dentsply Int'l, Inc.,* 277 F.Supp.2d 387, 453 (D.Del.2003) (quoting *LePage* s, *Inc. v. 3M,* 324 F.3d 141, 159 (3d Cir.2003)). Accordingly, the Court concluded that the Government had failed to establish violations of Section 3 of the Clayton Act and Sections 1 or 2 of the Sherman Act.

The Government appealed, contending that a monopolist that prevents rivals from distributing through established dealers has maintained its monopoly by acting with predatory intent and violates Section 2. Additionally, the Government asserts that the maintenance of a 75%--80% market share, establishment of a price umbrella, repeated aggressive price increases and exclusion of competitors from a major source of distribution, show that Dentsply possesses monopoly power, despite the fact that rivals are not entirely excluded from the market and some of their prices are higher. The Government did not appeal the rulings under Section 1 of the Sherman Act or Section 3 of the Clayton Act.

Dentsply argues that rivals had obtained a share of the relevant market, that there are no artificially high prices and that competitors have access to all laboratories through existing or readily convertible systems. In addition, Dentsply asserts that its success is due to its leadership in promotion and marketing and not the imposition of Dealer Criterion 6.

I. STANDARD OF REVIEW

We exercise *de novo* review over the District Court's conclusions of law. However, we will not disturb its findings of fact unless they are clearly erroneous.

II. APPLICABLE LEGAL PRINCIPLES

. . . A violation of Section 2 consists of two elements: (1) possession of monopoly power and (2) ". . . maintenance of that power as distinguished from growth or development as a consequence of a superior product, business acumen, or historic accident." *Eastman Kodak Co. v. Image Technical Servs. Inc.* 504 U.S. 451, 480 1992 (citing *United States v. Grinnell Corp.,* 384 U.S. 563, 571 (1966)). "Monopoly power under § 2 requires . . . something greater than market power under § 1" *Eastman Kodak Co.* 504 U.S. at 481.

To run afoul of Section 2, a defendant must be guilty of illegal conduct "to foreclose competition, gain a competitive advantage, or to destroy a competitor." *Id. at* 482-83. Behavior that otherwise might comply with antitrust law may be impermissibly exclusionary when practiced by a monopolist. As we said in *LePage's, Inc. v.* 3M, 324 F.3d 141, 151-52 (3d Cir.2003), "a monopolist is not free to take certain actions that a company in a competitive (or even oligopolistic) market may take, because there is no market constraint on a monopolist's behavior." 3 Areeda & Turner, *Antitrust Law* 813, at 300-02 (1978).

Although not illegal in themselves, exclusive dealing arrangements can be an improper means of maintaining a monopoly. *United States v. Grinnell Corp.*, 384 U.S. 563 (1966); *LePage s*, 324 F.3d at 157. A prerequisite for such a violation is a finding that monopoly power exists. *See, e.g., LePage's,* 324 F.3d at 146. In addition, the exclusionary conduct must have an anti-competitive effect. If those elements are established, the monopolist still retains a defense of business justification. *See id. at* 152.

Unlawful maintenance of a monopoly is demonstrated by proof that a defendant has engaged in anti-competitive conduct that reasonably appears to be a significant contribution to maintaining monopoly power. *United States v. Microsoft,* 253 F.3d 34, 79 (D.C.Cir.2001); 3 Phillip E. Areeda & Herbert Hovenkamp, *Antitrust Law,* ¶ 651c at 78 (1996). Predatory or exclusionary practices in themselves are not sufficient. There must be proof that competition, not merely competitors, has been harmed. *LePage's*, 324 F.3d at 162.

III. MONOPOLY POWER

. . . [T]he existence of monopoly power may be inferred from a predominant share of the market, *Grinnell* 384 U.S. at 571, and the size of that portion is a primary factor in determining whether power exists. *Pennsylvania Dental Assn v. Med. Serv. Assn of Pa., 745 F.2d 248, 260 (3d Cir.1984).*

A less than predominant share of the market combined with other relevant factors may suffice to demonstrate monopoly power. *Fineman v. Armstrong World Indus.,* 980 F.2d 171, 201 (3d Cir.1992). Absent other pertinent factors, a share significantly larger than 55% has been required to established prima facie market power. *Id.* at 201. Other germane factors include the size and strength of competing firms, freedom of entry, pricing trends and practices in the industry, ability of consumers to substitute comparable goods, and consumer demand.

A. The Relevant Market

Defining the relevant market is an important part of the analysis. The District Court found the market to be "the sale of prefabricated artificial teeth in the United States." *United States v. Dentply Int'l Inc.,* 277 F.Supp.2d 387, 396 (D.Del.2003). Further, the Court found that "[t]he manufacturers participating in the United States artificial tooth market historically have distributed their teeth into the market in one of three ways: (1) directly to dental labs; (2) through dental dealers; or (3) through a hybrid system combining manufacturer direct sales and dental dealers." The Court also found that the "labs are the relevant consumers for prefabricated artificial teeth."

There is no dispute that the laboratories are the ultimate consumers because they buy the teeth at the point in the process where they are incorporated into another product. Dentsply points out that its representatives concentrate their efforts at the laboratories as well as at dental schools and dentists.

During oral argument, Dentsply's counsel said, "the dealers are not the market . . . [t]he market is the dental labs that consume the product." Emphasizing the importance of end users, Dentsply argues that the District Court understood the relevant market to be the sales of artificial teeth to dental laboratories in the United States. Although the Court used the word "market" in a number of differing contexts, the findings demonstrate that the relevant market is not as narrow as Dentsply would have it. The Court said that Dentsply "has had a persistently high market share between 75% and 80% on a revenue basis, in the artificial tooth market." Dentsply sells only to dealers and the narrow definition of market that it urges upon us would be completely inconsistent with that finding of the District Court.

The Court went on to find that Ivoclar "has the second-highest share of the market, at approximately 5%." Ivoclar sells directly to the laboratories. Therefore, these two findings establish that the relevant market in this case includes sales to dealers and direct sales to the laboratories. Other findings on Dentsply's "market share" are consistent with this understanding.

These findings are persuasive that the District Court understood, as do we, the relevant market to be the total sales of artificial teeth to the laboratories and the dealers combined.

Dentsply's apparent belief that a relevant market cannot include sales both to the final consumer and a middleman is refuted in the closely analogous case of *Allen-Myland, Inc. v. IBM Corp.*, 33 F.3d 194 (3d Cir.1994). In that case, IBM sold mainframe computers directly to the ultimate consumers and also sold to companies that leased computers to ultimate users. We concluded that the relevant

60

market encompassed the sales directly to consumers as well as those to leasing companies. ". . . to the extent that leasing companies deal in used, non-IBM mainframes that have not already been counted in the sales market, these machines belong in the relevant market for large-scale mainframe computers." *Id. at* 203.

To resolve any doubt, therefore, we hold that the relevant market here is the sale of artificial teeth in the United States both to laboratories and to the dental dealers.

B. Power to Exclude

Dentsply's share of the market is more than adequate to establish a prima facie case of power. In addition, Dentsply has held its dominant share for more than ten years and has fought aggressively to maintain that imbalance. One court has commented that, "[i]n evaluating monopoly power, it is not market share that counts, but the ability to *maintain* market share." *United States v. Syufy Enters.,* 903 F.2d 659, 665-66 (9th Cir.1990).

The District Court found that it could infer monopoly power because of the predominant market share, but despite that factor, concluded that Dentsply's tactics did not preclude competition from marketing their products directly to the dental laboratories. "Dentsply does not have the power to exclude competitors from the ultimate consumer." *United States v. Dentsply Int'l, Inc.,* 277 F.Supp.2d 387, 452 (D.Del.2003).

Moreover, the Court determined that failure of Dentsply's two main rivals, Vident and Ivoclar, to obtain significant market shares resulted from their own business decisions to concentrate on other product lines, rather than implement active sales efforts for teeth.

The District Court's evaluation of Ivoclar and Vident business practices as a cause of their failure to secure more of the market is not persuasive. The reality is that over a period of years, because of Dentsply's domination of dealers, direct sales have not been a practical alternative for most manufacturers. It has not been so much the competitors' less than enthusiastic efforts at competition that produced paltry results, as it is the blocking of access to the key dealers. This is the part of the real market that is denied to the rivals.

The apparent lack of aggressiveness by competitors is not a matter of apathy, but a reflection of the effectiveness of Dentsply's exclusionary policy. Although its rivals could theoretically convince a dealer to buy their products and drop Dentsply's line, that has not occurred. In *United States v. Visa U.S.A.*. 344 F.3d at 229, 240 2d Cir.2003), the Court of Appeals held that similar evidence indicated that defendants had excluded their rivals from the marketplace and thus demonstrated monopoly power.

The Supreme Court on more than one occasion has emphasized that economic realities rather than a formalistic approach must govern review of antitrust activity. "Legal presumptions that rest on formalistic distinctions rather than actual market realities are generally disfavored in antitrust law . . . in determining the existence of market power . . . this Court has examined closely the economic reality of the market at issue." *Eastman Kodak Co. v. Image Technical Servs. Inc.* 504 U.S. 451, 466-67 (1992). "If we look at substance rather than form, there is little room for debate." *United States v. Sealy, Inc.,* 388 U.S. 350, 352 (1967). We echoed that standard in *Weiss v. York Hosp.,* 745 F.2d 786, 815 (3d Cir.1984). "Antitrust policy requires the courts to seek the economic substance of an arrangement, not merely its form." *Id.*

The realities of the artificial tooth market were candidly expressed by two former managerial employees of Dentsply when they explained their rules of engagement. One testified that Dealer Criterion 6 was designed to "block competitive distribution points." He continued, "Do not allow competition to achieve toeholds in dealers; tie up dealers; do not 'free up' key players."

Another former manager said:
You don't want your competition with your distributors, you don't want to give the distributors an opportunity to sell a competitive product. And you don't want to give your end user, the customer, meaning a laboratory and/or a dentist, a choice. He has to buy Dentsply teeth. That's the only thing that's available. The only place you can get it is through the distributor and the

only one that the distributor is selling is Dentsply teeth. That's your objective.

These are clear expressions of a plan to maintain monopolistic power.

The District Court detailed some ten separate incidents in which Dentsply required agreement by new as well as long-standing dealers not to handle competitors' teeth. For example, when the DLDS firm considered adding two other tooth lines because of customers' demand, Dentsply threatened to sever access not only to its teeth, but to other dental products as well. DLDS yielded to that pressure. The termination of Trinity Dental, which had previously sold Dentsply products other than teeth, was a similar instance. When Trinity wanted to add teeth to its line for the first time and chose a competitor, Dentsply refused to supply other dental products.

Dentsply also pressured Atlanta Dental, Marcus Dental, Thompson Dental, Patterson Dental and Pearson Dental Supply when they carried or considered adding competitive lines. In another incident, Dentsply recognized DTS as a dealer so as to "fully eliminate the competitive threat that [DTS locations] pose by representing Vita and Ivoclar in three of four regions."

The evidence demonstrated conclusively that Dentsply had supremacy over the dealer network and it was at that crucial point in the distribution chain that monopoly power over the market for artificial teeth was established. The reality in this case is that the firm that ties up the key dealers rules the market.

In concluding that Dentsply lacked the power to exclude competitors from the laboratories, "the ultimate consumers," the District Court overlooked the point that the relevant market was the "sale" of artificial teeth to both dealers and laboratories. Although some sales were made by manufacturers to the laboratories, overwhelming numbers were made to dealers. Thus, the Court's scrutiny should have been applied not to the "ultimate consumers" who used the teeth, but to the "customers" who purchased the teeth, the relevant category which included dealers as well as laboratories. This mis-focus led the District Court into clear error.

63

The factual pattern here is quite similar to that in *LePage's, Inc. v. 3M*, 324 F.3d 141 (3d Cir.2003). There, a manufacturer of transparent tape locked up high volume distribution channels by means of substantial discounts on a range of its other products. *LePage's*, 324 F.3d at 144, 160-62. We concluded that the use of exclusive dealing and bundled rebates to the detriment of the rival manufacturer violated Section 2. *See LePage's*, 324 F.3d at 159. Similarly, in *Microsoft*, the Court of Appeals for the D.C. Circuit concluded that, through the use of exclusive contracts with key dealers, a manufacturer foreclosed competitors from a substantial percentage of the available opportunities for product distribution. *See Microsoft*, 253 F.3d at 70-71.

The evidence in this case demonstrates that for a considerable time, through the use of Dealer Criterion 6 Dentsply has been able to exclude competitors from the dealers' network, a narrow, but heavily traveled channel to the dental laboratories.

C. Pricing

An increase in pricing is another factor used in evaluating existence of market power. Although in this case the evidence of exclusion is stronger than that of Dentsply's control of prices, testimony about suspect pricing is also found in this record.

The District Court found that Dentsply had a reputation for aggressive price increases in the market. It is noteworthy that experts for both parties testified that were Dealer Criterion 6 abolished, prices would fall. A former sales manager for Dentsply agreed that the company's share of the market would diminish should Dealer Criterion 6 no longer be in effect. In 1993, Dentsply's regional sales manager complained, "[w]e need to moderate our increases -- twice a year for the last few years was not good." Large scale distributors observed that Dentsply's policy created a high price umbrella.

Although Dentsply's prices fall between those of Ivoclar and Vita's premium tooth lines, Dentsply did not reduce its prices when competitors elected not to follow its increases. Dentsply's profit margins have been growing over the years. The picture is one of a manufacturer that sets prices with little concern for its competitors, "something a firm without a monopoly would have been unable to do." *Microsoft,* 253 F.3d at 58. The results have been favorable to Dentsply, but of no benefit to consumers.

Moreover, even "if monopoly power has been acquired or maintained through improper means, the fact that the power has not been used to extract [a monopoly price] provides no succor to the monopolist." *Microsoft,* 253 F.3d at 57 (quoting *Berkey Photo, Inc. v. Eastman Kodak, Co.,* 603 F.2d 263, 274 (2d Cir.1979)). The record of long duration of the exclusionary tactics and anecdotal evidence of their efficacy make it clear that power existed and was used effectively. The District Court erred in concluding that Dentsply lacked market power.

IV. ANTI-COMPETITIVE EFFECTS

Having demonstrated that Dentsply possessed market power, the Government must also establish the second element of a Section 2 claim, that the power was used "to foreclose competition." *United States v. Griffith,* 334 U.S. 100, 107 (1948). Assessing anti-competitive effect is important in evaluating a challenge to a violation of Section 2. Under that Section of the Sherman Act, it is not necessary that all competition be removed from the market. The test is not total foreclosure, but whether the challenged practices bar a substantial number of rivals or severely restrict the market's ambit. *LePage's,* 324 F.3d at 159-60; *Microsoft,* 253 F.3d at 69.

> A leading treatise explains,
> A set of strategically planned exclusive dealing contracts may slow the rival's expansion by requiring it to develop alternative outlets for its products or rely at least temporarily on inferior or more expensive outlets. Consumer injury results from the delay that the dominant firm imposes on the smaller rival's growth. Herbert Hovenkamp, *Antitrust Law* ¶ 1802c, at 64 (2d ed.2002).

By ensuring that the key dealers offer Dentsply teeth either as the only or dominant choice, Dealer Criterion 6 has a significant effect in preserving Dentsply's monopoly. It helps keep sales of competing teeth below the critical level necessary for any rival to pose a real threat to Dentsply's market share. As such, Dealer Criterion 6 is a solid pillar of harm to competition. *See LePage's*. 324 F.3d 141, 159 (3d Cir.2003) ("When a monopolist's actions are designed to prevent one or more new or potential competitors from gaining a foothold in the market by exclusionary, i.e. predatory, conduct, its success in that goal is not only injurious to the potential competitor but also to competition in general.").

A. Benefits of Dealers

Dentsply has always sold its teeth through dealers. Vita sells through Vident, its exclusive distributor and domestic affiliate, but has a mere 3% of the market. Ivoclar had some relationship with dealers in the past, but its direct relationship with laboratories yields only a 5% share.

A number of factors are at work here. For a great number of dental laboratories, the dealer is the preferred source for artificial teeth. Although the District Court observed that "labs prefer to buy direct because of potential cost savings attributable to the elimination of the dealer middleman [,]" in fact, laboratories are driven by the realities of the marketplace to buy far more heavily from dealers than manufacturers. This may be largely attributed to the beneficial services, credit function, economies of scale and convenience that dealers provide to laboratories, benefits which are otherwise unavailable to them when they buy direct.

The record is replete with evidence of benefits provided by dealers. For example, they provide laboratories the benefit of "one stop-shopping" and extensive credit services. Because dealers typically carry the products of multiple manufacturers, a laboratory can order, with a single phone call to a dealer, products from multiple sources. Without dealers, in most instances laboratories would have to place individual calls to each manufacturer, expend the time, and pay multiple shipping charges to fill the same orders.

The dealer-provided reduction in transaction costs and time represents a substantial benefit, one that the District Court minimized when it characterized "one stop shopping" as merely the ability to order from a single manufacturer all the materials necessary for crown, bridge and denture construction. Although a laboratory can call a manufacturer directly and purchase any product made by it, the laboratory is unable to procure from that source products made by its competitors. Thus, purchasing through dealers, which as a class traditionally carries the products of multiple vendors, surmounts this shortcoming, as well as offers other advantages.

Buying through dealers also enables laboratories to take advantage of obtaining discounts. Because they engage in price competition to gain laboratories' business, dealers often discount manufacturers' suggested laboratory price for artificial teeth. There is no finding on this record that manufacturers offer similar discounts.

Another service dealers perform is taking back tooth returns. Artificial teeth and denture returns are quite common in dentistry. Approximately 30% of all laboratory tooth purchases are returned for exchange or credit. The District Court disregarded this benefit on the ground that all manufacturers except Vita accept tooth returns. However, in equating dealer and manufacturer returns, the District Court overlooked the fact that using dealers, rather than manufacturers, enables laboratories to consolidate their returns. In a single shipment to a dealer, a laboratory can return the products of a number of manufacturers, and so economize on shipping, time, and transaction costs.

Conversely, when returning products directly to manufacturers, a laboratory must ship each vendor's product separately and must track each exchange individually. Consolidating returns yields savings of time, effort, and costs.

Dealers also provide benefits to manufacturers, perhaps the most obvious of which is efficiency of scale. Using select high-volume dealers, as opposed to directly selling to hundreds if not thousands of laboratories, greatly reduces the manufacturer's distribution costs and credit risks. Dentsply, for example, currently sells to twenty three dealers. If it were instead to sell directly to individual laboratories, Dentsply would incur significantly higher transaction costs, extension of credit burdens, and credit risks.

Although a laboratory that buys directly from a manufacturer may be able to avoid the marginal costs associated with "middleman" dealers, any savings must be weighed against the benefits, savings, and convenience offered by dealers.

In addition, dealers provide manufacturers more marketplace exposure and sales representative coverage than manufacturers are able to generate on their own. Increased exposure and sales coverage traditionally lead to greater sales.

B. "Viability" of Direct Sales

The benefits that dealers provide manufacturers help make dealers the preferred distribution channels -- in effect, the "gateways" -- to the artificial teeth market. Nonetheless, the District Court found that selling direct is a "viable" method of distributing artificial teeth. But we are convinced that it is "viable" only in the sense that it is "possible," not that it is practical or feasible in the market as it exists and functions. The District Court's conclusion of "viability" runs counter to the facts and is clearly erroneous. On the entire evidence, we are "left with the definite and firm conviction that a mistake has been committed." *United States v. Igbonwa,* 120 F.3d 437, 440 (3d Cir.1997).

It is true that Dentsply's competitors can sell directly to the dental laboratories and an insignificant number do. The undeniable reality, however, is that dealers have a controlling degree of access to the laboratories. The long-entrenched Dentsply dealer network with its ties to the laboratories makes it impracticable for a manufacturer to rely on direct distribution to the laboratories in any significant amount. *See United States v. Visa U.S.A.,* 344 F.3d 229, 240 (2d Cir.2003).

That some manufacturers resort to direct sales and are even able to stay in business by selling directly is insufficient proof that direct selling is an effective means of competition. The proper inquiry is not whether direct sales enable a competitor to "survive" but rather whether direct selling "poses a real threat" to defendant's monopoly. *See Microsoft,* 253 F.3d at 71. The minuscule 5% and 3% market shares eked out by direct-selling manufacturers Ivoclar and

Vita, Dentsply's "primary competitors," reveal that direct selling poses little threat to Dentsply.

C. Efficacy of Dealer Criterion 6

Although the parties to the sales transactions consider the exclusionary arrangements to be agreements, they are technically only a series of independent sales. Dentsply sells teeth to the dealers on an individual transaction basis and essentially the arrangement is "at-will." Nevertheless, the economic elements involved -- the large share of the market held by Dentsply and its conduct excluding competing manufacturers - realistically make the arrangements here as effective as those in written contracts. *See Monsanto Co. v. Spray-Rite Serv. Corp.,* 465 U.S. 752, 764 n. 9 (1984).

Given the circumstances present in this case, there is no ground to doubt the effectiveness of the exclusive dealing arrangement. In *LePage's,* 324 F.3d at 162, we concluded that 3M's aggressive rebate program damaged LePage's ability to compete and thereby harmed competition itself. LePage's simply could not match the discounts that 3M provided. *LePage's,* 324 F.3d at 161. Similarly, in this case, in spite of the legal ease with which the relationship can be terminated, the dealers have a strong economic incentive to continue carrying Dentsply's teeth. Dealer Criterion 6 is not edentulous.[62]

---

[62] In some cases which we find distinguishable, courts have indicated that exclusive dealing contracts of short duration are not violations of the antitrust laws. *See, e.g., CDC Techs., Inc. v. IDEXX Labs., Inc..* 186 F.3d 74, 81 (2d Cir.1999) ("distributors" only provided sales leads and sales increased after competitor imposed exclusive dealing arrangements); *Omega Envtl., Inc. v. Gilbarco. Inc.,* 127 F.3d 1157. 1163 (9th Cir.1997) (manufacturer with 55% market share sold both to consumers and distributors, market showed decreasing prices and fluctuating shares); *Rvko Mfg., Co. v. Eden Servs.,* 823 F.2d 1215 (8th Cir.1987) (manufacturer sold its products through direct sales and distributors); *Roland Mach. Co. v. Dresser Indus., Inc.,* 749 F.2d 380 (7th Cir.1984) (contract between dealer and manufacturer did not contain exclusive dealing provision).

D. Limitation of Choice

An additional anti-competitive effect is seen in the exclusionary practice here that limits the choices of products open to dental laboratories, the ultimate users. A dealer locked into the Dentsply line is unable to heed a request for a different manufacturers' product and, from the standpoint of convenience, that inability to some extent impairs the laboratory's choice in the marketplace.

As an example, current and potential customers requested Atlanta Dental to carry Vita teeth. Although these customers could have ordered the Vita teeth from Vident in California, Atlanta Dental's tooth department manager believed that they were interested in a local source. Atlanta Dental chose not to add the Vita line after being advised that doing so would cut off access to Dentsply teeth, which constituted over 90% ° of its tooth sales revenue.

Similarly, DLDS added Universal and Vita teeth to meet customers' requests, but dropped them after Dentsply threatened to stop supplying its product. Marcus Dental began selling another brand of teeth at one point because of customer demand in response to supply problems with Dentsply. After Dentsply threatened to enforce Dealer Criterion 6, Marcus dropped the other line.

E. Barriers to Entry

Entrants into the marketplace must confront Dentsply's power over the dealers. The District Court's theory that any new or existing manufacturer may "steal" a Dentsply dealer by offering a superior product at a lower price, *see Omega Environmental. Inc. v. Gilbarco.* 127 F.3d 1157 (9th Cir.1997), simply has not proved to be realistic. To the contrary, purloining efforts have been thwarted by Dentsply's longtime, vigorous and successful enforcement actions. The paltry penetration in the market by competitors over the years has been a refutation of theory by tangible and measurable results in the real world.

The levels of sales that competitors could project in wooing dealers were minuscule compared to Dentsply's, whose long-standing relationships with these dealers included sales of other dental products. For example, Dentsply threatened Zahn with termination if it started selling Ivoclar teeth. At the time, Ivoclar's projected $1.2 million in sales were 85% lower than Zahn's $8 million in Dentsply's sales.

When approached by Leach & Dillon and Heraeus Kulzer, Zahn's sales of Dentsply teeth had increased to $22-$23 million per year. In comparison, the president of Zahn expected that Leach & Dillon would add up to $200,000 (or less than 1% of its Dentsply's sales) and Heraeus Kulzer would contribute "maybe hundreds of thousands." Similarly, Vident's $1 million in projected sales amounted to 5.5% of its $18 million in annual Dentsply's sales.

The dominant position of Dentsply dealers as a gateway to the laboratories was confirmed by potential entrants to the market. The president of Ivoclar testified that his company was unsuccessful in its approach to the two large national dealers and other regional dealers. He pointed out that it is more efficient to sell through dealers and, in addition, they offered an entre to future customers by promotions in the dental schools.

Further evidence was provided by a Vident executive, who testified about failed attempts to distribute teeth through ten identified dealers. He attributed the lack of success to their fear of losing the right to sell Dentsply teeth.

Another witness, the president of Dillon Company, advised Davis, Schottlander & Davis, a tooth manufacturer, "to go through the dealer network because anything else is futile. . . . Dealers control the tooth industry. If you don't have distribution with the dealer network, you don't have distribution." Some idea of the comparative size of the dealer network was illustrated by the Dillon testimony: "Zahn does $2 billion, I do a million-seven. Patterson does over a billion dollars, I do a million-seven. I have ten employees, they have 6,000."

Dealer Criterion 6 created a strong economic incentive for dealers to reject competing lines in favor of Dentsply's teeth. As in *LePage's*, the rivals simply could not provide dealers with a comparable economic incentive to switch. Moreover, the record demonstrates that Dentsply added Darby as a dealer "to block Vita from a key competitive distribution point." According to a Dentsply executive, the "key issue" was "Vita's potential distribution system." He explained that Vita was "having a tough time getting teeth out to customers. One of their key weaknesses is their distribution system."

Teeth are an important part of a denture, but they are but one component. The dealers are dependent on serving all of the laboratories' needs and must carry as many components as practicable. The artificial teeth business cannot realistically be evaluated in isolation from the rest of the dental fabrication industry.

> A leading treatise provides a helpful analogy to this situation: [S]uppose that mens's bow ties cannot efficiently be sold in stores that deal exclusively in bow ties or even ties generally; rather, they must be sold in department stores where clerics can spread their efforts over numerous products and the ties can be sold in conjunction with shirts and suits. Suppose further that a dominant bow tie manufacturer should impose exclusive dealing on a town's only three department stores. In this case the rival bow tie maker cannot easily enter. Setting up another department store is an unneeded and a very large investment in proportion to its own production, which we assume is only bow ties, but any store that offers less will be an inefficient and costly seller of bow ties. As a result, such exclusive dealing could either exclude the nondominant bow tie maker or else raise its costs in comparison to the costs of the dominant firm. While the department stores might prefer to sell the ties of multiple manufacturers, if faced with an "all-or-nothing" choice they may accede to the dominant firm's wish for exclusive dealing. Herbert Hovenkamp, *Antitrust Law* ¶ 1802e3, at 78-79 (2d ed.2002).

Criterion 6 imposes an "all-or-nothing" choice on the dealers. The fact that dealers have chosen not to drop Dentsply teeth in favor of a rival's brand demonstrates that they have acceded to heavy economic pressure.

This case does not involve a dynamic, volatile market like that in *Microsoft*, 253 F.3d at 70, or a proven alternative distribution channel. The mere existence of other avenues of distribution is insufficient without an assessment of their overall significance to the market. The economic impact of an exclusive dealing arrangement is amplified in the stagnant, no growth context of the artificial tooth field.

Dentsply's authorized dealers are analogous to the high volume retailers at issue in *LePage's*. Although the dealers are distributors and the stores in *LePage's*, such as K-Mart and Staples, are retailers, this is a distinction in name without a substantive difference. *LePage's*, 324 F.3d at 144. Selling to a few prominent retailers provided "substantially reduced distribution costs" and "cheap, high volume supply lines." *Id.* at 160 n. 14. The manufacturer sold to a few high volume businesses and benefitted from the widespread locations and strong customer goodwill that prominent retailers provided as opposed to selling directly to end-user consumers or to a multitude of smaller retailers. There are other ways across the "river" to consumers, but high volume retailers provided the most effective bridge.

The same is true here. The dealers provide the same advantages to Dentsply, widespread locations and long-standing relationships with dental labs, that the high volume retailers provided to 3M. Even orders that are drop-shipped directly from Dentsply to a dental lab originate through the dealers. This underscores that Dentsply's dealers provide a critical link to end-users.

Although the District Court attributed some of the lack of competition to Ivoclar's and Vident's bad business decisions, that weakness was not ascribed to other manufacturers. Logically, Dealer Criterion 6 cannot be both a cause of the competitors' lower promotional expenditures which hurt their market positions, and at the same time, be unrelated to their exclusion from the marketplace. Moreover, in *Microsoft*, in spite of the competitors' self-imposed problems, the Court of Appeals held that Microsoft possessed monopoly power because it benefitted from a significant barrier to entry. *Microsoft*, 253 F.3d at 55.

Dentsply's grip on its 23 authorized dealers effectively choked off the market for artificial teeth, leaving only a small sliver for competitors. The District Court erred when it minimized that situation and focused on a theoretical feasibility of success through direct access to the dental labs. While we may assume that Dentsply won its preeminent position by fair competition, that fact does not permit maintenance of its monopoly by unfair practices. We conclude that on this record, the Government established that Dentsply's exclusionary policies and particularly Dealer Criterion 6 violated Section 2.

V. BUSINESS JUSTIFICATION

As noted earlier, even if a company exerts monopoly power, it may defend its practices by establishing a business justification. The Government, having demonstrated harm to competition, the burden shifts to Dentsply to show that Dealer Criterion 6 promotes a sufficiently pro-competitive objective. *United States v. Brown Univ.,* 5 F.3d 658, 669 (3d Cir.1993). Significantly, Dentsply has not done so. The District Court found that "Dentsply's asserted justifications for its exclusionary policies are inconsistent with its announced reason for the exclusionary policies, its conduct enforcing the policy, its rival suppliers' actions, and dealers' behavior in the marketplace."

Some of the dealers opposed Dentsply's policy as exerting too much control over the products they may sell, but the grandfathered dealers were no less efficient than the exclusive ones, nor was there any difference in promotional support. Nor was there any evidence of existence of any substantial variation in the level of service provided by exclusive and grandfathered dealers to the laboratories.

The record amply supports the District Court's conclusion that Dentsply's alleged justification was pretextual and did not excuse its exclusionary practices.

VI. AVAILABILITY OF SHERMAN ACT SECTION 2 RELIEF

One point remains. Relying on *dicta* in *Tampa Electric Co. v. Nashville Coal Co.,* 365 U.S. 320 (1961), the District Court said that

74

because it had found no liability under the stricter standards of Section 3 of the Clayton Act, it followed that there was no violation of Section 2 of the Sherman Act. However, as we explained in *LePage's* v. 3M, 324 F.3d at 157 n. 10, a finding in favor of the defendant under Section 1 of the Sherman Act and Section 3 of the Clayton Act, did not "preclude the application of evidence of . . . exclusive dealing to support the [Section 2 claim." All of the evidence in the record here applies to the Section 2 claim and, as in *LePage's*, a finding of liability under Section 2 supports a judgment against defendant. . . . Here, the Government can obtain all the relief to which it is entitled under Section 2 and has chosen to follow that path without reference to Section 1 of the Sherman Act or Section 3 of the Clayton Act. We find no obstacle to that procedure.

CHAPTER 9: MERGERS

Insert after *Heinz*, page 1080

NOTE

United States v. *Oracle Corp.*, 331 F. Supp. 2d 1098 (D.C. Cal. 2004). In 2004, the Department of Justice and 10 states sought a preliminary injunction to block Oracle Corporation from acquiring People Soft, Inc., two companies that manufactured and sold a type of application software that automated business data processing ("EAS"). Programs that provide EAS functions include human relations management ("HRM"), financial management systems ("FMS"), customer relations management, supply chain management, product life cycle management, and business intelligence, among many others. The government claimed that the combination of the HRM and FMS functions, and then only at the high end of those two application systems, constituted a relevant market. One other large company - SAP - (like Oracle and People Soft) offered a comprehensive set of software, and many other companies offered specific sets of software to the market.

The case depended largely on relevant product market definition, and that issue in turn depended upon what various witnesses testified about the ability of the combined firms to raise price after the proposed merger.

In support of their proposed product market definition, the government presented at trial or through depositions 10 customer witnesses, five industry witnesses, two systems integration witnesses, three expert witnesses, and a few others who according to the court appeared mostly to fill a gap or two in the evidence or to supply "spice" for the record. Typically, competitor testimony has been regarded as suspect because rivals may be comfortable with the idea of a merger that leads to higher prices, which would lead to higher profits for all competitors in the market. On the other hand, customer evidence has in the past been regarded as fairly persuasive. The District Court, in denying a preliminary injunction, took a different view of the customer evidence in this particular case. After summarizing witness testimony, the Court concluded:

Plaintiffs' Evidence of a High Function HRM & FMS
Market

... The court will not attempt to recount or even summarize the entire evidentiary record. Given the quantity of evidence, that would be unduly time-consuming and is unnecessary. It suffices to note that the laboring oar of the plaintiffs' case was pulled by the customer witnesses (whom plaintiffs' counsel described as their strongest witnesses), by some of the systems integrator and industry witnesses and by the experts.

[Gorriz of Daimler testified]: Daimler has about 365,000 employees worldwide in about 100 manufacturing facilities. Since 1996, Daimler has used SAP as its financial management software. Daimler requires highly functional HRM to accommodate its large number of employees and to comply with the differing labor laws and union agreements in different countries. For its HRM needs, Daimler currently uses PeopleSoft. Daimler chose PeopleSoft based upon its reputation and the fact that companies of comparable size to Daimler have had success with PeopleSoft HRM. But when Daimler was first searching for an HRM vendor in 1996, Gorriz stated that "only SAP, PeopleSoft or Oracle could serve [Daimler's] needs for the HR management." Gorriz stated that Daimler considered no other vendors. Daimler's legacy system was "too old" for the company seriously to consider upgrading. Daimler did not consider outsourcing to be an option because Daimler's HRM requirements were, Gorriz testified, "too complex." Further, if Oracle, SAP or PeopleSoft were to increase their price for HRM by 10 percent, Gorriz stated that Daimler "would not consider any offer" from any other vendors.

Bob Bullock, Senior Vice President and Chief Information Officer of CH2M Hill, testified about the ERP needs of that civil and environmental engineering firm. CH2M Hill has 14,000 employees, 200 worldwide offices and over $2 billion in annual revenue. CH2M Hill has used Oracle FMS since 1993, but in 2002 the company decided to replace its legacy HRM software. Bullock stated that through consultation with the Gartner Group, CH2M Hill was given a list of HRM vendors. CH2M Hill did not seriously consider SAP, as it "was a very complex product" and had a "reputation for being a costly product." In Bullock's opinion, there were only two candidates, Oracle and PeopleSoft. CH2M Hill never considered outsourcing, Lawson or remaining on its legacy system. Oracle and PeopleSoft both offered initial bids between $1.5 and 41.6 million. Bullock stated that if this price had been 10 percent higher, CH2M Hill would not walked away from the deal with Oracle or PeopleSoft.

Curtis Wolfe, CIO for the State of North Dakota, testified about the state's process of picking an ERP vendor. North Dakota has approximately 10,000 full and part-time employees, 58 state agencies and a budget of $5 billion. In 2002, the state decided to buy a full ERP program that included FMS and HRM. North Dakota had a unique need in that it required that its ERP serve the state's higher education facilities as well. *Id.* North Dakota had six vendors submit proposals: Oracle, PeopleSoft, SAP, SCT, Jenzabar (a partner of Lawson) and Microsoft's Great Plains. The state eliminated SAP, Great Plains and Jenzabar almost immediately. SAP was too expensive, while Jenzabar and Great Plains did not have the required functionality. SCT did not make the final round; while SCT met the functionality for the higher education area, it could not do so with state agency needs. Oracle and PeopleSoft were in head to head competition and Wolfe testified that he believes that this caused the state to get a $6 to $8 million lower final bid from each vendor. If these final offers had been 10 percent higher, Wolfe stated that North Dakota would not have turned to Lawson, Microsoft, SCT, outsourcing or writing its own software.

Kenneth Johnsen, Chief of Technology for Pepsi Americas, testified as to his concerns about the Oracle/PeopleSoft merger. Pepsi Americas is the second largest bottler of Pepsi-brand soft drinks within the Pepsi system and the third largest bottler worldwide. Pepsi Americas has over 15,000 employees and annual revenues of about $3.2 billion. Pepsi Americas uses PeopleSoft ERP in its North America operations and SAP ERP in its European operations. Johnsen testified that he has "a concern" about the impact of this merger on the long-term effectiveness of the PeopleSoft ERP. Johnsen is concerned that a post-merger Oracle, while agreeing to maintain the PeopleSoft ERP, will not provide enhancements to the functionality of the software (i.e., upgrades). To Johnsen this leaves Pepsi Americas with two options: constantly upgrade with point solutions (not his desired choice) or buy ERP from a new vendor. When asked, what vendors he could turn to meet his ERP needs, Johnsen claims there are no options outside of Oracle, PeopleSoft and SAP.

Scott Wesson, Senior Vice President and Chief Information Officer of AIMCO, discussed the company's choices for FMS and HRM software. AIMCO is the largest owner and operator of apartment buildings in the United States. The company owns approximately 2000 complexes in 47 states and the District of Columbia. AIMCO has over 6,500 employees and an annual revenue of about $1.5 billion. For its FMS, AIMCO uses PeopleSoft's financial suite. For its HR payroll systems, AIMCO currently uses Lawson. In 2002, AIMCO began to reevaluate its HRM options and it hired Towers Perrin consult in this process. Towers Perrin told AIMCO that only three vendors could meet AIMCO's HRM needs: PeopleSoft, Oracle and SAP. (There was no objection to the question that elicited this response). Wesson stated that AIMCO decided not to upgrade to the latest version of Lawson because it would have cost AIMCO "about the same * * * as it would to go with a new system" and also, Lawson "[was] lacking some key features" that AIMCO was looking for. AIMCO was deciding between Oracle and PeopleSoft when Oracle first made its tender offer to PeopleSoft. Wesson stated that because of this proposed merger, he believes PeopleSoft gave him a "very good deal" on the HRM. Wesson testified that Oracle agreed to match any price offered by PeopleSoft. Wesson said AIMCO ultimately chose PeopleSoft because PeopleSoft had guaranteed to pay AIMCO three times the contract price should there be a "change of ownership" at PeopleSoft. AIMCO is expecting to implement the PeopleSoft system in late 2004 or early 2005. Moreover, Wesson stated, AIMCO does not consider outsourcing to be a viable option because it is not quick to respond to "last minute changes," such as new benefits programs. Best of breed solutions are too expensive for AIMCO to consider.

Richard Cichanowicz, Vice President of Systems Integration of Nextel, testified about the wireless services company's ERP needs.

Nextel has 13 million subscribers, over $8 billion in annual revenue 17,000 [transcript incorrect] employees. Before 2002, Nextel had been using PeopleSoft HRM, Oracle FMS and Ariba SCM. In 2002, however, Nextel determined that using one integrated solution would provide more operational efficiency. Nextel received advice from six consulting firms, which informed Nextel that Oracle, SAP and PeopleSoft could meet those software needs. Nextel then sent RFPs to Oracle and Peoplesoft. Nextel did not seriously consider SAP because it was already using Oracle for FMS and PeopleSoft for HRM and believed that conversion costs and risks for those two vendors would be lower. Nextel ultimately chose Peoplesoft, based on its scoring of vendor criteria such as functionality, ease of integration, scalability, audits, costs and relationship confidence. Even after it had chosen PeopleSoft, however, Nextel continued to negotiate with Oracle for leverage purposes until the signing of the December 2002 contract with PeopleSoft. Cichanowicz stated that if the price of the Oracle or PeopleSoft licenses had been 10 percent higher, Nextel would not have considered a best of breed approach, writing or building its own ERP software, outsourcing, staying with its previous system or using SAP or any other United States vendor.

Mary Elizabeth Glover, Vice President of Information Technology at Greyhound Lines, testified about her company's foray into the market for HRM software. Greyhound is in the bus transportation business in both the United States and Canada. The company employees some 16,000 people and has annual revenues of around $1.2 billion. For its FMS, Greyhound uses Oracle in the United States and J D Edwards in Canada. For its HRM, Greyhound uses a product called HR1 in the United States and HR2000 in Canada. The company outsources its payroll to ADP. Glover stated that the HR incumbent systems are "very old" and no longer meet the needs of the company. Further, she testified that outsourcing is too expensive for Greyhound. For these reasons, in 2001, Greyhound began a potential procurement process for new HRM software. The company hired CDG & Associates to match Greyhound with potential vendors who met their HRM needs. The firm narrowed the selection down to only four vendors: Oracle, PeopleSoft, Lawson and Ultimate Software. Greyhound never considered SAP because the consulting firm believed they were too costly. Ultimate Software was eliminated soon thereafter because of lack of functionality. Greyhound eliminated PeopleSoft as being too costly. Between Oracle and Lawson, Greyhound found that Oracle had more functionality; therefore, Lawson was eliminated. But before Greyhound made a final choice, Glover stated that the company decided to give PeopleSoft a second look. Upon reexamination, Greyhound determined that both Oracle and PeopleSoft could meet the company's needs, with the company preferring PeopleSoft over Oracle. Unfortunately, the events of September 11, 2001, a new CEO and a decrease in profits caused Greyhound to lose the funds necessary to purchase the software. But Glover stated that should Greyhound ever decide to purchase HRM software, this proposed merger would make the purchase more costly, as Greyhound's only choices were Oracle and PeopleSoft. Without the competition between the two, Glover foresees prices increasing.

Phillip Maxwell, Senior Vice President and Chief Information Officer of the Neiman Marcus Group (NMG), testified about the ERP needs of the specialty retailer. NMG has properties located throughout the country, approximately 15,000 employees and $3 billion in annual sales. NMG formerly had used FMS software that was originally from MSA, a vendor purchased by Dun & Bradstreet and then GEAC subsequent to NMG's installation of the software. In 2002, NMG decided to replace its FMS software and began conferring with individuals in its business and technology units, three consulting firms and the Gartner Group. After examining vendors' functionality, experience in retail, price and size/stability, NMG narrowed its choices to Oracle and PeopleSoft. NMG did not consider SAP because of SAP's lack of strong presence in the retail vertical and Maxwell's opinion that SAP is "very expensive to implement." Had the cost of Oracle or PeopleSoft FMS software been 10 to 20 percent higher, NMG would not have considered SAP, any other FMS vendor, legacy software or internally developed software. Based on price, a high level comparison and detailed GAP analysis, NMG eventually selected Oracle to provide it with FMS software.

NMG also began licensing HRM software from Oracle in 2003, though it has not yet begun to implement that software. NMG went through a similar process in evaluating HRM software as it did in evaluating FMS software. As with the FMS software, NMG

81

concluded that Oracle and PeopleSoft were its only viable alternatives. NMG did not believe that SAP suited its needs as a retailer. Had the cost of the Oracle or PeopleSoft HRM software been 10 to 20 percent higher, NMG would not have considered other HRM vendors, legacy software, internally developed software or outsourcing. NMG eventually selected the Oracle HRM software, but based on a 70 to 80 percent higher target price than previously predicted, NMG has delayed implementation of the Oracle HRM software to look for cost-reducing options. But Maxwell testified that, even with the 80 percent price increase, NMG has not abandoned the Oracle HRM.

Laurette Bradley, Senior Vice President of Information Technology at Verizon, testified about Verizon's current procurement of new HRM software. Verizon is a telecommunications company with a "majority holding in four of five different countries." Verizon has minor investments in over 30 countries worldwide with an annual revenue of approximately $66 billion. *Id.* Bradley testified that 49 percent of Verizon's labor is unionized worldwide, which places "significant demands upon [the] ERP systems, particularly [the] HR and payroll systems" because each union contract, from each jurisdiction, must be reflected and managed regarding payroll, vacation, absences, and personal days. Prior to October 2003, Verizon had used two different HRM programs, one from PeopleSoft and one from SAP. The PeopleSoft HRM was used to manage the former BellAtlantic part of the company and SAP HRM was used to manage the former GTE part of the company. The same is true of Verizon's FMS. But in October 2003, Verizon decided to consolidate the two systems as far as HRM software. Verizon chose PeopleSoft HRM for the entire company and as of the date of the trial, the new software was being implemented. *Id.* Bradley testified that a merger between Oracle and PeopleSoft makes her very concerned that Oracle will not be interested in upgrading or further "developing" current PeopleSoft software.

In the main, and contrary to the characterization of plaintiffs' counsel before trial, the court found the testimony of the customer witnesses largely unhelpful to plaintiffs' effort to define a narrow market of high function FMS and HRM. Each of these witnesses had an impressive background in the field of information technology.

They appeared knowledgeable and well informed about their employers' ERP needs and resources. And the court does not doubt the sincerity of these witnesses' beliefs in the testimony that they gave. What the court questions is the grounds upon which these witnesses offered their opinions on the definition of the product market and competition within that market.

The test of market definition turns on reasonable substitutability. *E. I. du Pont,* 351 U.S. 377, 76 S.Ct. 994, 100 L.Ed. 1264. This requires the court to determine whether or not products have "reasonable interchangeability" based upon "price, use and qualities * * *." What, instead, these witnesses testified to was, largely, their preferences.

Customer preferences towards one product over another do not negate interchangeability. See *R R Donnelley & Sons Co.,* 120 FTC 36, 54 n. 65 (1995) (citing Robert Pitofsky, *New Definitions of the Relevant Market and the Assault on Antitrust,* 90 Colum. L. Rev. 1805, 1816 (1990) ("There will almost always be classes of customers with strong preferences * * * but to reason from the existence of such classes to a conclusion that each is entitled to * * * a separate narrow market definition grossly overstates the market power of the sellers.")). The preferences of these customer witnesses for the functional features of PeopleSoft or Oracle products was evident. But the issue is not what solutions the customers would *like* or *prefer* for their data processing needs; the issue is what they *could* do in the event of an anticompetitive price increase by a post-merger Oracle. Although these witnesses speculated on that subject, their speculation was not backed up by serious analysis that they had themselves performed or evidence they presented. There was little, if any, testimony by these witnesses about what they would or could do or not do to avoid a price increase from a post-merger Oracle. To be sure, each testified, with a kind of rote, that they would have no choice but to accept a ten percent price increase by a merged Oracle/PeopleSoft. But none gave testimony about the cost of alternatives to the hypothetical price increase a post-merger Oracle would charge: e.g., how much outsourcing would actually cost, or how much it would cost to adapt other vendors' products to the same functionality that the Oracle and PeopleSoft products afford.

If backed by credible and convincing testimony of this kind or testimony presented by economic experts, customer testimony of the kind plaintiffs offered can put a human perspective or face on the injury to competition that plaintiffs allege. But unsubstantiated customer apprehensions do not substitute for hard evidence.

While listening to the testimony of these customer witnesses, it became clear to the court that these witnesses represent a group of extremely sophisticated buyers and users of information technology; they have decades of experience in negotiating in this field. This made more evident the failure of these witnesses to present cost/benefit analyses of the type that surely they employ and would employ in assessing an ERP purchase. The evidence at trial established that ERP customers have choices outside the integrated suites of Oracle, PeopleSoft and SAP. Indeed, Glover's testimony showed that - as Oracle contends - customers have some leverage by virtue of their existing installed base "to do nothing" and thereby resist anticompetitive price increases by ERP vendors. Although the court is not convinced that this is a long-term option due to the ever changing business and legal environment in which enterprises operate, this option does afford ERP customers some limited protection and leverage. At any rate, plaintiffs' customer witnesses did not, in their testimony, provide the court with data from actual or probable ERP purchases and installations to demonstrate that the witnesses' employers would have had no choice but to submit to a SSNIP imposed by a post-merger Oracle.

The court, therefore, finds that these witnesses did not establish by a preponderance of the evidence that the products offered by Oracle, PeopleSoft and SAP are in a distinct line of commerce or product market from those offered by other ERP vendors. The court finds that these witnesses did not establish that it was more likely than not that customers of a post-merger Oracle would have no choice but to submit to a small but significant non-transitory price increase by the merged entity. These findings do not rest alone on the court's skepticism about the testimony of plaintiffs' customer witnesses.

*   *   *

In the concluding sections of the opinion, the Court turned to questions of likely anticompetitive effects as the result of collusive behavior or unilateral effects. Largely on the basis of the government's failure to establish relevant product market on the basis of consumer testimony or otherwise, the government's request for an injunction was denied.

CHAPTER 9: MERGERS

Insert after Note 6, page 1090

DAGHER v. SAUDI REFINING AND MOTIVA ENTERPRISES

United States Court of Appeals, Ninth Circuit, 2004

369 F. 3d 1108

REINHARDT, J. Plaintiffs Fouad N. Dagher, et al., appeal from the district court's award of summary judgment to the defendants, Texaco, Inc., Shell Oil Co., and Saudi Refining, Inc. (SRI), et al. The plaintiffs represent a class of 23,000 Texaco and Shell service station owners who allege that the defendants conspired to fix the nationwide prices for the Shell and Texaco brands of gasoline through the creation of a national alliance consisting of two joint ventures. The district court granted two summary judgment motions: one to dismiss defendant SRI because the plaintiffs lacked antitrust standing; the other to dismiss the complaint against the remaining defendants because the plaintiffs failed to raise a triable issue of fact as to whether the Sherman Antitrust Act's *per se* prohibition against price fixing is applicable to the economic arrangements between the defendants. We affirm the district court's ruling as to the plaintiffs' standing to sue SRI, but reverse the district court's decision that the plaintiffs failed to create a triable issue of fact under the Sherman Act.

I.   Factual and Procedural History

        A.   Factual History

        Texaco, Inc., and Shell Oil Co. were once fierce competitors in the national oil and gasoline markets. They competed at both wholesale and retail levels, and in both upstream and downstream operations.[63] The two companies generally operated by

---

[63]   The parties have explained in their joint stipulations that "[c]rude oil is the raw product from which gasoline is made at a refinery.

Footnote continued on next page

independently refining gasoline and then selling the gas either to licensed Texaco and Shell service stations or to wholesale distributors.

From 1989 to 1998, defendants Saudi Refining, Inc. (SRI) and Texaco sold gas on the East Coast through Star Enterprise, a joint venture "engaged in the refining and marketing of gasoline under the Texaco brand." Both Shell and Texaco sensed intensified competition in the downstream operations of their industry - they similarly believed that "the oil industry was about to enter a period of consolidation." To respond to the heightened competition in the oil and gas industry, Shell approached Texaco in 1996 about several potential corporate combinations designed to enhance efficiency and reduce competition between the two companies with respect to the downstream refining and marketing of gasoline. In 1998, preliminary discussions yielded an agreement to form a nationwide alliance (hereinafter: "the alliance")[64] consisting of two separate joint

---

Footnote continued from previous page
Upstream operations consist of exploring for and producing crude oil, and down-stream operations consist of refining crude into gasoline and other products and marketing the finished products."

[64] Defendants dispute that an "alliance" existed and characterize Equilon and Motiva as distinct entities. While the defendant corporations did not create a new legal entity called "The Alliance," the record establishes beyond dispute that representatives of Texaco and Shell generally referred to the two joint ventures as part of a single project to combine the two companies' nationwide refining and marketing operations. Moreover, the record confirms that the single project was often referred to as "an alliance," and frequently called "The Alliance," by representatives of Texaco, Shell, and SRI, and by Board Members from the two joint ventures, "Equilon Enterprises" (Equilon) and "Motiva Enterprises" ('Motiva). When we refer to "the alliance," we therefore refer to the combined national refining and marketing operation consisting of Equilon and Motiva - an enterprise which was created, developed, and maintained collectively by the individual defendant corporations.

87

ventures.[65]   One joint venture was named "Equilon Enterprises" (Equilon); it combined Shell's and Texaco's downstream operations in the western United States. The other venture, formed by Texaco, Shell, and SRI, was named "Motiva Enterprises" (Motiva); it combined the three companies' downstream operations in the eastern United States. The alliance had a national market share of 15% of all gasoline sales, and on the West Coast, Equilon's market share exceeded 25%.

There is a voluminous record documenting the economic justifications for creating the joint ventures. After analysis by teams made up of representatives of all three companies, the defendants concluded that numerous synergies and cost efficiencies would result. The defendants concluded that nationwide there would be up to $800 million in cost savings annually. The Federal Trade Commission and several State Attorneys General approved the formation of the joint ventures, subject to modifications demanded by both the federal agency and the various Attorneys General.

The creation of the alliance ended competition between Shell and Texaco throughout the nation in the areas of downstream refining and marketing of gasoline. Texaco and Shell signed non-competition agreements which prohibited them from competing with either Equilon or Motiva and committed them "not to engage in the manufacturing and marketing of certain products in the [relevant] geographic area[s], including fuel, synthetic gasoline, and electricity." The two joint ventures established fixed ratios for profit sharing and for bearing the risk of losses. In Equilon, Shell has a 56% interest while Texaco owns 44%. In Motiva, Shell owns 35%, while SRI and Texaco each own 32.5%.

Despite the collective assumption of risk and resource pooling in the joint ventures, Shell and Texaco continued to operate as distinct

---

[65]   The district court explained the massive scope of the alliance: "[t]he downstream assets in Equilon and Motiva include twelve refineries, twenty-three lubricant plants, two research laboratories, 22,000 branded service stations, over 24,000 miles of pipeline, 107 terminals, and approximately 24,000 employees."

corporations. Each retained its own trademarks and kept control over its own brands pursuant to separate Brand Management Protocols, each of which prohibited the joint ventures from giving preferential treatment to either brand. Under the joint venture agreements, Equilon and Motiva market Shell and Texaco gasoline under licensing agreements governing both the sale of the products and the use of the Shell and Texaco trademarks. Each company maintained its ability to return to individual sales and marketing - the joint ventures contain provisions allowing for dissolution at any time by mutual consent or, after five years time, by unilateral dissolution with two years advance notice.

The various agreements between the oil companies allowed Texaco and Shell to consolidate and unify the pricing of the Texaco and Shell gasoline brands within the Equilon and Motiva joint ventures. Before creating the two joint ventures, Shell, Texaco, and Star all independently set prices for their wholesale and retail sales, generally through decisions made by their corporate pricing units. Testimony in the record reveals that, either immediately before the formation of the joint ventures or sometime shortly thereafter, "a decision was made that the Shell and Texaco brands would have the same price in the same market areas." The decision to charge the same price for the two distinct brands "was developed as sort of an operating requirement right from the very start or near to the very start of the alliance." Equilon and Motiva integrated this pricing decision into a project named "The Strategic Marketing Initiative" (SMI), which sought to develop ways in which the alliance could produce and promote both brands more competitively. There is some evidence in the record establishing that the decision to set one price for the two brands was conceived of in the SMI even before Motiva was formed.[66]

---

[66] The record does not establish with certainty whether the decision to price the two brands together was actively discussed during the SMI. The evidence does show that the SMI included a "price optimization" program. And there is some evidence in the record that the price optimization program ratified the unofficial decision to move toward unitary pricing -- one witness testified that the price

Footnote continued on next page

The alliance consolidated pricing of the Texaco and Shell brands such that a single individual at each joint venture was responsible for setting a coordinated price for the two brands. The joint ventures did, however, continue to adjust the pegged price of the brands to each unique geographic sale area. The pricing was consolidated despite the fact that Texaco and Shell maintained each brand as a distinct product -- each brand has its own unique chemical composition (the gasoline is differentiated by separate packages of "additives"), trademark, and marketing strategy -- and competed for customers "at the pump." The companies, and the joint ventures, continued to target each brand at a different customer base -- "Texaco customers tend to be more blue-collared and rural than Shell customers, who are more affluent and urban."

The price optimization program may have allowed Equilon and Motiva to raise gasoline prices at a time when the price of crude oil was low and stable. During a time when crude oil prices reached near-historic lows -- the price of crude oil decreased from $12 to $10 per barrel between September 1998 and February 1999 -- Equilon raised its prices $.40 per gallon in Los Angeles and $.30 per gallon in both Seattle and Portland.

B.   Procedural History

The plaintiffs commenced this civil action in the United States District Court for the Central District of California. They brought suit on behalf of themselves and approximately 23,000 Shell and Texaco service station owners, alleging that defendants SRI, Texaco, Shell, Motiva, Equilon, Equiva Trading Co., and Equiva Services, LLC, engaged in a price fixing scheme to raise and fix gas prices through the alliance and the two joint ventures, Motiva and Equilon, in violation of Section 1 of the Sherman Antitrust Act, 15 U.S.C. § 1. The plaintiffs disclaimed any reliance on the traditional "rule of

---

Footnote continued from previous page
optimization program included "a policy or a procedure to charge the same prices to both -- to similar classes of trade in the same marketing areas and to effect those -- to effect those changes."

90

reason" test, instead resting their entire claim on either the per se rule or a "quick look" theory of liability.

The defendants moved to dismiss under Fed. R, Civ. P. 12(b)(6). The issue with respect to the 12(b)(6) motion was "whether the alleged agreement among Saudi, Shell, and Texaco is an unreasonable restraint of trade . . . under either the *per se* rule or a 'quick look' rule of reason analysis." The district court denied the motion. The court found that although the *per se* rule against price fixing plainly does not make all price-restraining joint ventures illegal, neither does "[a]n agreement to fix prices . . . merit full rule of reason treatment solely because it is part of a broader joint venture agreement." The court explained that "price fixing can still be illegal *per se* even if it accompanies an efficient, integrated joint venture. If the joint venture could function perfectly well without price fixing, then the price fixing amounts to no more than an extraneous, anticompetitive restraint that does not merit rule of reason analysis." The district court found that the plaintiffs' complaint alleged sufficient facts to demonstrate that the alliance's price setting regime was a naked, rather than an ancillary, restraint on trade.[67] The district court disposed of the plaintiffs' alternative theories of liability -- the plaintiffs originally alleged a "market division" theory and a "manipulation of leases" theory to support their *per se* Section 1 violation -- but gave plaintiffs leave to amend.

The parties filed cross-motions for summary judgment. The district court decided the motions in two separate orders. The first order granted SRI's motion for summary judgment on the ground that the plaintiffs lacked antitrust standing because no plaintiff had ever bought gasoline, or other products, from the Motiva joint venture or directly from SRI and because the plaintiffs lacked "direct or circumstantial evidence 'sufficiently unambiguous to permit a trier of fact to find that [SRI] conspired' to fix prices in the western United

---

[67]   A "horizontal agreement [is] 'naked' if it is formed with the objectively intended purpose or likely effect of increasing price or decreasing output in the short run, with output measured by quantity or quality."   XI HERBERT HOVENKAMP, ANTITRUST LAW ¶ 1905, at 210(1998) (hereinafter: HOVENKAMP).

91

States absent 'any apparent motive to do so.' " (citing *Matsushita Elec. Indus. Co. v. Zenith Radio Corp.*, 475 U.S. 574, 597, 106 S. Ct. 1348, 89 L.Ed.2d 538 (1986)).

The second order granted the remaining defendants' motion for summary judgment on the ground that the rule of reason, not the *per se* or "quick look" rules, governed the Sherman Act analysis of the joint ventures. The district court applied its own analytical framework, consisting of two questions: "(1) whether a reasonable trier of fact could conclude that Equilon and Motiva are either mere window-dressings for a price fixing conspiracy or (2) whether they are otherwise patently anticompetitive." The court concluded -- relying on the detailed and costly negotiations leading up to the creation of the joint ventures -- that Equilon and Motiva were plainly not "fly-by-night" operations designed to cover up an elaborate price-fixing scheme. Moreover, the court found that Motiva and Equilon produced sufficient efficiencies and were sufficiently integrated to constitute indisputably legitimate joint ventures under either the *per se* rule or a "quick look" analysis. Finally, the district court concluded that, because every joint venture "must, at some point, set prices for the products they sell" (citation omitted), a theory which made it illegal for a joint venture to fix prices of its various brands would "act as a per se rule against joint ventures companies that produce competing products."

II.   Standard of Review

We review a district court's grant of summary judgment *de novo*. *United States v. City of Tacoma*, 332 F.3d 574, 578 (9th Cir. 2003). Taking the evidence in the light most favorable to the nonmovant, we must consider whether there are any genuine issues of material fact and whether the district court properly applied the pertinent substantive law. . . . As the Supreme Court explained in *Poller v. Columbia Broadcasting Sys, Inc.,* 368 US, 464, 82 S. Ct. 486, 7 L.Ed.2d 458 (1962):

> [S]ummary procedures should be used
> sparingly in complex antitrust litigation
> where motive and intent play leading
> roles, the proof is largely in the hands of

the alleged conspirators, and hostile witnesses thicken the plot. It is only when the witnesses are present and subject to cross-examination that their credibility and the weight to be given their testimony can be appraised.

Id. at 473, 82 S. Ct. 486.

III.   Standing

The district court found that the plaintiffs lacked standing to sue SRI. The court's decision was based upon two considerations: first, none of the named plaintiffs had ever purchased any products from SRI or from Motiva; and second, the plaintiffs failed to produce sufficient evidence linking SRI to a conspiracy to fix prices in the Western United States. There is no dispute that the plaintiffs never purchased any products from SRI, or from Motiva. Nor is there any doubt that SRI did not sign any of the documents establishing Equilon, did not refine or market gasoline in the Western United States, and had no motive to conspire with Shell and Texaco to fix those brands' prices in the West. Yet the plaintiffs maintain that SRI engaged in a nationwide price-fixing conspiracy with Texaco and Shell through its participation in Motiva, and therefore is liable for all of the acts of each conspiracy member. *See Beltz Travel*, 620 F.2d at 1367; *see also Appellants' Brief, at* 42.

The plaintiffs rest their theory of standing on the existence of a national conspiracy -- and, in this case, defendants Texaco, Shell, Equilon, and Motiva have admitted that they fixed prices by charging the same price for the Texaco and Shell brands. But the plaintiffs do not establish standing under our precedent simply by showing that SRI was involved to some extent in the planning of certain aspects of the alliance. Rather, "[f]or an agreement to constitute a violation of section 1 of the Sherman Act, a 'conscious commitment to a common scheme designed to achieve an unlawful objective' must be established." *Toscano v. PGA*, 258 F.3d 978, 983 (9th Cir. 2001) (quoting *Monsanto Co. v. Spray-Rite Serv. Corp.*, 465 U.S. 752, 764, 104 S. Ct. 1464, 79 L.Ed.2d 775 (1984)).

The plaintiffs did proffer evidence showing that Equilon and Motiva were formed as the result of a series of negotiations designed to create a national alliance. Apparently, Shell originally approached the other parties with "ideas about a larger alliance" and explored the possibility of a nationwide alliance. The record contains clear evidence showing that Equilon and Motiva were conceived of as a single strategy to create a national operating structure, separated solely for the sake of efficiency. Moreover, the plaintiffs point to substantial evidence that Equilon and Motiva made pricing decisions together via cooperation through their marketing departments.

Still, the plaintiffs have failed to provide evidence sufficiently implicating SRI in the nationwide price-fixing scheme. The district court found that SRI had "no apparent motive to conspire with Shell and Texaco with respect to Equilon and the Western United States," largely because SRI "would not benefit from any potential anticompetitive effects in Equilon's territory." The plaintiffs have offered no evidence to the contrary. In fact, the record shows unequivocally that SRI's interests were limited to the operation of Motiva and the refining and marketing of gasoline in the Eastern portion of the nation, and that, even there, SRI vigorously protested the domination of the Motiva Board by Shell and Texaco representatives. SRI lamented that the Motiva Board members, who were corporate representatives of Texaco and Shell, and many of whom were also members of the Equilon Board, appeared to be making their decisions for the nationwide "alliance" rather than for the individual joint ventures.[68] The record thus demonstrates that --

---

[68] One board member who represented SRI in Motiva observed that, "once the Equilon Board takes a position on an issue common to both Motiva and Equilon, Shell and Texaco will have a strong desire to have the same action taken in Motiva." The member furth er stated:

> As is exhibited by Motiva's incorrect reference to the Alliance, rather than Motiva, at the bottom of page 7 and the top of page 8 of the attached Business Plan writeup, the 'focus on Motiva' message will have to be repeated often to get it accepted. The more we allow "Alliance" to dominate, the greater the likelihood that

Footnote continued on next page

far from engaging in a nationwide conspiracy -- SRI had little interest in acceding to the "cooperative" efforts by "common Motiva and Equilon Board members, from Shell and Texaco." In short, the plaintiffs failed to produce evidence that SRI had a "conscious commitment to a common scheme designed to achieve an unlawful objective." *Monsanto*, 465 U.S. at 764, 104 S. Ct. 1464. Although the issue is a close one, we affirm the district court's holding that the plaintiffs failed to establish that SRI participated in the operation of a nationwide price-fixing alliance or in the fixing of prices in the Western region of the United States.

IV.   Liability under the Sherman Antitrust Act

"No antitrust violation is more abominated than the agreement to fix prices. With few exceptions, 'price-fixing agreements are unlawful *per se* under the Sherman Act and . . . no showing of so-called competitive abuses or evils which those agreements were designed to eliminate or alleviate may be interposed as a defense.' The dispositive question generally is not whether any price fixing was justified, but simply whether it occurred." *Freeman v. San Diego Ass'n of Realtors*, 322 F.3d 1133._1144 (9th Cir.2003). The question we confront in this case, however, is not whether two companies engaged in run-of-the-mill price fixing. Instead, the defendants have asked us to find an exception to the *per se* prohibition on price-fixing where two entities have established a joint venture that unifies their production and marketing functions, yet continue to sell their formerly competitive products as distinct brands. In doing so, the companies fixed the prices of those two brands of gasoline, Texaco and Shell, by agreeing *ex ante* to charge the exact same price for each. We think the exception the defendants seek is inconsistent with the Sherman Act as it has been understood to date.

Footnote continued from previous page
> personal behavior will favor "Alliance" over Motiva and the greater the likelihood that sub-optimizations of Motiva, in favor of the Alliance, will occur. We are on alert in this regard but the "Alliance" force is a large one.

The Sherman Antitrust Act makes illegal "[e]very contract, combination in the form of trust or otherwise, or conspiracy, in restraint of trade or commerce among the several States, or with foreign nations[.]" 15 U.S.C. § 1. The Supreme Court has declined to read this language literally. *See Nat'l Soc'y of Prof'l Engineers v. United States*, 435 U.S. 679, 687. 98_S. Ct. 1355, 55 L.Ed.2d 637 (1978) (noting that § 1 of the Sherman Act "cannot mean what it says"). Instead, the Court has created a two-tiered mode of analysis.

> In the first category are agreements whose nature and necessary effect are so plainly anticompetitive that no elaborate study of the industry is needed to establish their illegality -- they are "illegal *per se*." In the second category are agreements whose competitive effect can only be evaluated by analyzing the facts peculiar to the business, the history of the restraint, and the reasons why it was imposed. In either event, the purpose of the analysis is to form a judgment about the competitive significance of the restraint; it is not to decide whether a policy favoring competition is in the public interest, or in the interest of members of an industry. Subject to exceptions defined by statute, that policy decision has been made by the Congress.

Prof'l Engineers, 435 U.S. at 692, 98 S. Ct. 1355. All parties agree that the relevant question in this case is whether the defendants' conduct falls under the first category of analysis.[69]

---

[69] The plaintiffs have also suggested that if we reject their *per se* approach, we should employ the "quick look" theory of review to find defendants liable. Quick look analysis applies when *per se* review is inapplicable but when "an observer with even a rudimentary

Footnote continued on next page

If the plaintiffs can establish that the defendants' conduct falls within the range of conduct considered illegal *per se*, it does not matter whether the particular application of the *per se* rule appears inefficient or unfair. As the Court has explained,

> The costs of judging business practices under the rule of reason, however, have been reduced by the recognition of per se rules. Once experience with a particular kind of restraint enables the Court to predict with confidence that the rule of reason will condemn it, it has applied a conclusive presumption that the restraint is unreasonable. As in every rule of general application, the match between the presumed and the actual is imperfect. For the sake of business certainty and litigation efficiency, we have tolerated the invalidation of some agreements that a fullblown inquiry might have proved to be reasonable.

Footnote continued from previous page
understanding of economics could conclude that the arrangements in question have an anti-competitive effect on customers and markets." *California Dental Ass'n v. Federal Trade Commission*, 526 U.S. 756, 770, 119 S. Ct. 1604, 143 L.Ed.2d 935 (1999). As the district court rightly noted, "[m]uch like per se treatment, quick-look analysis applies 'when the great likelihood of anticompetitive effects can easily be ascertained.' " (quoting *California Dental*, 526 U.S. at 770, 119, S. Ct. 1604). Because we hold that the plaintiffs have made a sufficient showing with respect to the illegality of the alliance's price fixing system under the *per se* rule, we need not decide whether that scheme would survive "quick look" review.

Arizona v. Maricopa County Med. Soc'y, 457 U.S. 332, 343-44, 102 S. Ct. 2466, 73 L.Ed.2d 48 (1982) (citations omitted).[70] The Court has held consistently that the injustice of the rule's broad and uniform application must be addressed to Congress, not the judiciary. *See Prof'l Engineers*, 435 U.S. at 692, 98 S. Ct. 1355.

Price fixing is the quintessential example of a *per se* violation of § 1. Numerous cases support this basic principle.

. . .

Notwithstanding the above, it is plain that § 1's blanket prohibition on price fixing, like the Act itself, cannot be read literally. *Cf. Prof'l Engineers*, 435 U.S. at 687, 98 S. Ct. 1335 (§ 1 of the Sherman Act "cannot mean what it says"). There are some price fixing arrangements that violate the letter of the Sherman Act but are legal nonetheless. For instance, when two competing companies agree to merge and to combine their product lines, or to eliminate the old product lines and create an entirely new one, they generally agree to adopt a uniform pricing scheme. The Supreme Court has permitted such arrangements. In addition, in *Maricopa County*, the Supreme Court noted in dicta that in joint ventures where "persons who would otherwise be competitors pool their capital and share the risks of loss as well as the opportunities for profit," the ventures are considered, for some purposes at least, to be "single firm[s] competing with other sellers in the market." 457 U.S. at 356, 102 S. Ct. 2466; *see also Broad. Music, Inc. v. Columbia Broad Svs. Inc.*, 441 U.S. 1, 9, 99 S. Ct. 1551, 60 L.Ed.2d 1 (1979) ("When two partners set the price of their goods or services they are literally 'price fixing,' but they are not per se in violation of the Sherman Act.") hereinafter: *BMI*) (citation omitted).

---

[70] The *Maricopa* Court noted in a footnote that price fixing is "[a]mong the practices which the courts have heretofore deemed to be unlawful in and of themselves." *Id.* at 344 n. 15, 102 S. Ct. 2466 (quoting *Northern Pac. R. Co. v. United States*, 356 U.S. 1, 5, 78 S. Ct. 514, 2 L.Ed.2d 545 (1958)) (parallel citation omitted).

It is not the case, however, that the mere existence of a bona fide joint venture means that participating companies may use the enterprises to do anything they please with full immunity from *per se* analysis under § 1, including price fixing. As the district court correctly stated when ruling on the motion to dismiss, the issue with respect to legitimate joint ventures is whether the price faxing is "naked" (in which case the restraint is illegal) or "ancillary" (in which case it is not). *Accord* XI HOVENKAMP ¶ 1908, at 228-30 (arguing that "a restraint does not qualify as 'ancillary' merely because it accompanies some other agreement that is itself lawful" and that "a restraint is not saved from the 'naked' classification simply because it is included in some larger joint venture arrangement that is clearly efficient"). For instance, if in reliance on the existence of a valid joint venture between Coca Cola and Pepsi designed to research new types of soda flavors, the two companies imposed a price floor on all soda sold nationwide, the price fixing would constitute an illegal "naked restraint on trade." Along these lines, the Supreme Court has recognized that even joint ventures that are lawful in their general operations may violate the Sherman Act when they engage in specific anticompetitive conduct. *See NCAA*, 468 U.S. at 110, 104 S. Ct. 2948 (holding that an agreement among NCAA schools restricting the broadcasting of football games was an invalid "naked restraint on price and output" but not questioning the validity of the association itself); *BMI*, S. Ct. at 23, 99 S. Ct. 1551 (holding that joint ventures are not "*usually* unlawful, at least not . . . where the agreement on price is necessary to market the product at all") (emphasis added); *Timken Roller Bearing Co. v. United States*, 341 U.S. 593, 598, 71 S. Ct. 971, 95 L.Ed. 1199 (1951) ("The fact that there is common ownership or control of the contracting corporations does not liberate them from the impact of the antitrust laws. . . . [A]greements between legally separate persons and companies to suppress competition among themselves and others [cannot] be justified by labeling the project a 'joint venture.' ") (citation omitted); *see also* XI HOVENKAMP ¶ 1908, at 228-29 (1998) (noting that the Supreme Court has often condemned joint ventures' price- or output-fixing provisions while leaving "the balance of the joint venture intact").

The defendants argument to the contrary -- that joint ventures such as Equilon and Motiva are incapable of violating the Sherman

Act - ignores the lesson of *Citizen Publishing Co. v. United States*, 394 U.S. 131, 89 S. Ct. 927, 22 L.Ed.2d 148 (1969), as well as that of *NCAA*, *BMI*, and *Timken*. In *Citizen Publishing*, the Supreme Court confronted a joint venture similar to the one between Equilon and Motiva. The defendants in that case were the two daily newspapers in Tucson, Arizona. They entered into a joint venture agreement, which "provided that each paper should retain its own news and editorial departments, as well as its corporate identity." The joint venture established a new company, Tucson Newspapers, Inc., "which was to manage all departments of their business except the news and editorial units. The production and distribution equipment of each paper was transferred to TNI." *Id.* at 133-34. 89 S. Ct. 927. The purpose of the agreement, like the purpose of the Alliance, was "to end any business or commercial competition between the two papers."[71]

The Supreme Court held that the confluence of these anticompetitive restraints, in the context of a joint venture between two formerly-vigorous competitors in the market area targeted by the venture, constituted a *per se* violation of the Sherman Act.

> The § 1 violations are plain beyond peradventure. Price-fixing is illegal per se. Pooling of profits pursuant to an inflexible ratio at least reduces incentives to compete for circulation and advertising revenues and runs afoul of the Sherman Act. The agreement not to engage in any other publishing business in Pima County was a division of fields also banned by the Act. The

---

[71] Also similar to the agreements forming Equilon and Motiva, the *Citizen Publishing* agreement imposed several anticompetitive controls: first, the joint venture consolidated pricing and set joint subscription and advertising rates; second, the venture pooled all profits and losses pursuant "to an agreed ratio"; and third, the two parent corporations agreed not to compete against each other or the joint venture in the relevant market areas. *Id.*

> joint operating agreement exposed the
> restraints so clearly and unambiguously
> as to justify the rather rare use of a
> summary judgment in the antitrust field.

Id. at 135. 139 S. Ct. 927 (internal citations omitted). Cases like *Maricopa County* and *BMI* do seem to suggest that the Court, if confronted with a similar joint venture today, might not find the enterprise as a whole unlawful. The Court has, however, continued to enforce the Sherman Act's *per se* prohibition on price fixing, and has scrutinized joint ventures to ensure that they do not contain "naked" restraints on trade. *See, e.g., NCAA*, 468 U.S. at 109, 104 S. Ct. 2948. Nothing in the cases suggests that the Court would overrule *Citizen Publishing* in its entirety, abandon its holding that the price fixing in which the joint venture engaged was illegal *per se*, or eliminate the rule that "naked" price-fixing by a joint venture violates the Sherman Act.

The district court distinguished *Citizen Publishing* in three ways. Each is unsatisfactory. First, the court found that the Tucson newspapers in *Citizen Publishing* effectively eliminated "all competition," whereas Equilon and Motiva "continue to compete with several major oil companies in their relevant markets." This distinction runs contrary to Supreme Court precedent. *See Fed. Trade Comm'n*, 493 U.S. at 434, 436, 110 S. Ct. 768 (noting that even "a small conspirator may be able to impede competition" and holding that "[c]onspirators need not achieve the dimensions of a monopoly, or even a degree of market power any greater than that already disclosed by this record, to warrant condemnation under the antitrust laws").[72]

Second, the district court found that the *Citizen Publishing* newspapers "combined for the specific purpose of restricting

---

[72]   *See also NCAA*, 468 U.S. at 109-10, 104 S. Ct. 2948 ("As a matter of law, the absence of proof of market power does not justify a naked restraint on price or output. . . . This naked restraint on price and output requires some competitive justification even in the absence of a detailed market analysis.").

competition and fixing prices," in contrast to a complete lack of evidence establishing such intent for the alliance ventures. That distinction, if true, would speak only to the validity of Equilon and Motiva as a whole-it would not justify the defendants' adoption of a price fixing scheme. Moreover, the court's finding was contrary to its obligation to accept the version of disputed facts most favorable to the plaintiffs. Several of the defendants' witnesses admitted during depositions that the decision to unify the pricing of the Texaco and Shell brands was made contemporaneously with the formation of the alliance, but before the actual joint ventures officially existed, and that the very purpose of the alliance was to eliminate competition in order to realize efficiency gains and gain market share.[73] The plaintiffs created a sufficient issue of material fact as to whether the intended purpose of the unified pricing scheme was to restrict competition.

Third, the district court believed that the only reason the non-competition agreement in *Citizen Publishing* was unlawful was

_____

[73] Thus, contrary to our dissenting colleague's understanding, the pricing decision was not made by a single economic entity. See Post, at 1126, *id.* at 1127 ("[N]othing more radical is afoot than the fact that an entity, which now owns all of the production, transportation, research, storage, sales and distribution facilities for engaging in the gasoline business, also prices its own products. It decided to price them the same, as any other entity could."). At this stage of the litigation, we are required to draw all reasonable inferences in favor of the plaintiffs. Viewing the evidence in that light, there is at least a triable issue of fact as to whether Texaco and Shell agreed in advance to charge the same price for their two distinct gasoline brands as an initial operating requirement of the alliance. The decision by Texaco and Shell to include in their joint ventures a unified pricing scheme was not a decision made by a single economic entity - it was a decision made by competitors. Whether the agreement constituted "a conspiracy [ ] in restraint of trade," 15 U.S.C. § 1, or whether such a conspiracy would exist regardless of when the decision to engage in unified pricing was made, is for the district court to determine on remand.

because the agreement joined the only two competitors in the market. The Western oil market, by contrast, is a diverse market with "several competitors," while the Equilon joint venture has a much narrower non-competition agreement. This distinction returns to an analysis of market power, an analysis which the Supreme Court has held is inappropriate in this type of case. *See Federal Trade Comm'n,* 493 U.S. at 434-35, 110 S. Ct. 768; *NCAA,* 468 U.S. at 110, 104 S. Ct. 2948 ("We have never required proof of market power in such a case."). Moreover, the record shows both that Equilon exercised a substantial amount of control over the Western gasoline market, and that the two joint ventures helped divide the gasoline consumer field by jointly promoting and targeting the Texaco and Shell brands to better capture their relevant markets. None of the district court's distinctions is sufficient to justify ignoring *Citizen Publishing* and that decision's condemnation of price fixing by former competitors even when adopted as part of a joint venture arrangement.

In granting the defendants' summary judgment motion, the district court ruled that "a reasonable trier of fact could not find that the Defendants formed Equilon and Motiva merely to achieve an ulterior anticompetitive purpose or that the ventures are patently anticompetitive."[74] Even were that true, the district court stopped short of completing the requisite inquiry. The proper inquiry for a *per se* analysis of price fixing is not simply whether the joint venture itself is anticompetitive. Nor is the relevant question simply whether the defendants intended to destroy competition. *See Paladin Associates. Inc. v. Montana Power Co.,* 328 F.3d 1145, 1153-54 (9th Cir. 2003) (holding that evidence of an intent to destroy competition or engage in predatory price controls is not essential to demonstrating the existence of an illegal agreement). Rather, if the answer to those questions is in the negative, we must then decide whether the defendants' conduct -- setting one, unified price for both the Texaco and Shell brands of gasoline instead of setting each brand's price

---

[74] The district court asked whether "Equilon and Motiva are either mere window-dressings for a price fixing conspiracy or . . . are otherwise patently anticompetitive."

independently on the basis of normal market factors[75] --is reasonably necessary to further the legitimate aims of the joint venture. *See Freeman,* 322 F.3d at 1151, (holding that plainly anticompetitive conduct by otherwise valid joint ventures must be "reasonably ancillary to the legitimate cooperative aspects of the venture").

The Supreme Court has upheld joint ventures and other corporate combinations involving fixed prices, but generally has done so only when it appeared plain to the Court that the restraints undertaken by the joint ventures were "necessary" to the legitimate aims of the joint venture. *See BMI,* 441 U.S. at 23, 99 S. Ct. 1551 (approving an otherwise invalid price restraint only because "the agreement on price is necessary to market the product at all"); *NCAA,* 468 U.S. at 117, 104 S. Ct. 2948 ("Our decision not to apply a per se rule to this case rests in large part on our recognition that a certain degree of cooperation is necessary if the type of competition that petitioner and its member institutions seek to market is to be preserved."); *id.,* at 101, 104 S. Ct. 2948 ("what is critical is that this case involves an industry in which horizontal restraints on competition are essential if the product is to be available at all"); *accord* XI HOVENKAMP ¶ 1908, at 236 ("Joint sales endeavors may require joint price setting, particularly when the jointly produced product, such as the 'blanket' license in *BMI,* is something individual participants could not produce at all."). Courts have engaged in this "essentiality query," in order to ensure that a joint venture has a legitimate justification - other than the desire to enhance profits and market control - for adopting a particular restraint that would otherwise violate the Sherman Act. Thus, whether the *per se* rule applies to a legitimate joint venture's allegedly anticompetitive conduct depends first and foremost on a determination of whether the specific restraint is sufficiently important to attaining the lawful objectives of the joint venture that the anti-competitive effects should be disregarded.[76]

---

[75]   We assume that normal market factors would include the cost of production and marketing, supply, demand, and the like.

[76]   As one commentator has explained,

Footnote continued on next page

104

In considering the relationship of the enterprise's pricing actions to the venture's legitimate objectives, we find it significant that the defendants here did not simply consolidate the pricing decisions within the joint ventures -- they *unified* the pricing of the two brands from the time the alliance was formed by designating one individual in each joint venture to set a single price for both brands.[77] Normally, a business determines the prices it will charge for its various products by considering numerous factors, just a few of which include the costs of production and marketing and the contours of the relevant product markets. In this case, the defendants have stressed that, in addition to the differences in the product themselves, the gasolines marketed under the Texaco and Shell labels have different reputations and consumer bases. It thus seems likely that independent price analyses would result, at least in some circumstances, in the

---

Footnote continued from previous page

> Once a court finds the joint venture proper, it can easily determine the appropriateness of any related competitive restraints among the parties to the venture. A court should simply consider whether such restraints are necessary to promote the venture's procompetitive purposes. If a joint venture itself is procompetitive, the courts should uphold any restrictions on competition necessary to achieve its legitimate purposes. . . . The defendant should have the burden of proving that a competitive restraint is required to further a venture's efficiency objectives. If a defendant fails to meet this burden, a court should preclude the restraint without any further inquiry.

Thomas A. Piraino, Jr., *A Proposed Antitrust Approach to Collaborations Among Competitors*, 86 Iowa L. Rev. 1137, 1188-89 (2001).

[77] As stated earlier, this single price was subject to variations depending upon geographic markets, such that the price of the Texaco and Shell brands might be higher in San Diego, California than it was in Lincoln, Nebraska. The two brands, however, were always priced together in each geographic market -- the price never varied as between the two.

rational decision to sell the different brands at different prices. Instead, the defendants chose to fix those prices uniformly.

The defendants have thus far failed to offer any explanation of how their unified pricing of the distinct Texaco and Shell brands of gasoline served to further the ventures' legitimate efforts to produce better products or capitalize on efficiencies. Nor does the record contain facts sufficient to warrant our drawing any such inference. To the contrary, the record before us reveals that the alliance never considered unified pricing to be relevant to product improvement or efficiency gains. As one oil company executive explained, all of the anticipated cost savings, which were calculated prior to formation of the joint ventures, had "nothing to do with pricing." The absence of persuasive evidence showing a procompetitive justification for initiating the price-fixing scheme, when viewed along with the plaintiffs' evidence showing anticompetitive effects, convinces us that the plaintiffs have made a sufficient showing as to the applicability of the *per se* rule.[78]

The defendants offer only two justifications for the unitary pricing scheme. First, the defendants argue -- as does our dissenting colleague -- that, as a general rule, any bona fide joint venture must be able to set prices for its products at whatever level it chooses: "without the ability to price its products, neither venture would have had the authority to make fundamental decisions affecting its financial performance." Appellees' Brief, at 16. Second, the defendants argue that Equilon and Motiva fixed uniform Texaco and Shell prices in order to "prevent issues of price discrimination from arising under the Robinson Patman Act[.]" *Id.* We address the latter justification first.

---

[78] Indeed, the record is close to establishing that the price-fixing scheme was sufficiently unrelated to accomplishing the legitimate objectives of the joint venture as to justify granting the plaintiffs' motion for summary judgment. However, given the complexity of the economic arrangements at issue, the sparseness of the record, the district court's failure to apply the appropriate test, and our general presumption against granting summary judgment in such cases, we conclude that the denial of both sides' motion for summary judgment is appropriate here.

A cursory examination of the Robinson-Patman Act, 15 U.S.C. § 13,[79] which was designed to prevent sellers from engaging in price discrimination, reveals its inapplicability here. Under Robinson Patman, sellers may not sell the same product at different prices on the basis of the identity of the buyer.[80] But in adopting the Act, "Congress did not intend to outlaw price differences that result from or further the forces of competition." *Brooke Group Ltd. v. Brown & Williamson Tobacco Corp.*, 509 U.S. 209, 220, 113 S. Ct. 2578, 125 L.Ed.2d 168 (1993). . . .

The Act would unquestionably be inapplicable to a decision by the defendants to sell the distinct Texaco and Shell brands of gasoline at different prices. Any such decision would necessarily be predicated on the differences between the two brands, not upon the identity of the buyers. The record shows that the alliance never intended to market or sell the two brands as the same product. Rather, it went to great lengths to differentiate carefully between the brands. Mostly, this took place at the additive stage -- where generic "fungible" gasoline is transformed into a specific brand. But it also took place at the marketing stage, where the Texaco and Shell brands of gasoline were always targeted at different groups of consumers. The defendants cite no precedent or provision of statutory law that would support applying Robinson Patman to a decision to use different prices for distinct, though similar, products. Finally, this Circuit has rejected "the argument relying on the 'underlying notion of fairness of offering the same services at the same prices to all participants.' The 'fairness' of uniform pricing is not a relevant consideration in an antitrust case; consumers are presumed to prefer

---

[79] The Act provides that "[i]t shall be unlawful for any person engaged in commerce, in the course of such commerce, either directly or indirectly, to discriminate in price between different purchasers of commodities of like grade and quality[.]" 15 U.S.C. § 13(a).

[80] The Act explicitly excludes price differentials "which make only due allowance for differences in the cost of manufacture, sale, or delivery resulting from the differing methods or quantities in which such commodities are to such purchasers sold or delivered[.]" 15 U.S.C. 13(a).

lower prices to the satisfaction of knowing they paid the same inflated price as everyone else." *Freeman*, 322 F.3d at 1151.

The first of the defendants' two arguments -- that a joint venture must be able to set whatever price it chooses for its products -- proves too much. If that were true, any number of companies could create joint ventures as fronts for price-fixing. The simple answer is that the Supreme Court has declined to immunize joint ventures from *per se* antitrust scrutiny. *See NCAA*. 468 U.S. at 109, 104 S, Ct. 2948; *BMI*, 441 U.S. at 23, 99 S. Ct._1551; *Citizen Publishing*, 394 U.S. at 135, 89 S. Ct. 927, *Timken*, 341 U.S. at 598, 71 S. Ct. 971. We too have rejected the plaintiffs' proposed rule. *See Freeman* 322 F.3d at 1148 (holding that the fact that joint ventures "pursue the common interests of the whole" does not necessarily immunize them from antitrust scrutiny and noting that "cases finding joint ventures to be incapable of conspiracy are the 'exception' "). The leading treatise in the field has also expressed similar disapproval of the defendants' claim. *See* XI HOVENKAMP ¶ 1908, at 229 ("Such a rule could protect cartels from the heightened scrutiny attending naked restraints through the simple device of attaching the cartel agreement to some other, independently lawful transaction.").

Finally, the defendants claim - as does our dissenting colleague - that an application of the *per se* rule here would mean that joint ventures could not set prices for their products. We reject this argument. We of course recognize that joint ventures may price their products; that is not the question. The question is whether two former (and potentially future) competitors may create a joint venture in which they unify the pricing, and thereby *fix* the prices, of two of their distinct product brands. We have held that the Sherman Act's *per se* rule applies when the defendant fails to demonstrate a sufficient relationship between the price fixing scheme and furthering the legitimate aims of the joint venture - a relationship that justifies the otherwise prohibited price restraints. Thus far in this litigation, the defendants have failed to produce sufficient evidence demonstrating that their price fixing scheme was ancillary rather than naked and, thus, that they are entitled to summary judgment.

The result we reach here allows joint ventures to set prices for their products within the limits of the Sherman Act. Our analysis would be different if we confronted a joint venture in which former competitors agreed jointly to research, produce, market, and sell a new product, or a joint venture in which competitors agreed to merge their current product lines into one collective brand. Nor would we necessarily reach the same result if the defendants had independently decided to charge the same price for Texaco and Shell gasoline after conducting separate price analyses for each brand, or had they come forward with persuasive evidence that the setting of a single, fixed price was important to accomplishing the legitimate aims of the joint ventures.

We do not share the defendants' concern that validating the application of the *per se* rule to the pricing decisions of joint ventures will risk invalidating countless economically efficient business integrations. The plaintiffs have come forward with sufficient evidence to create a triable issue of fact as to whether the defendants engaged in a naked restraint on trade, prohibited *per se* by the Sherman Act. Whether the defendants will be found liable at trial remains to he seen. But if they are, and if that individual application of the *per se* rule is economically inefficient, that concern must be addressed to Congress, not the judiciary. *See Maricopa County*, 457 U.S. at 354-55. 102 S. Ct. 2466; *Professional Engineers*, 435 U.S. at 692, 98 S. Ct. 1355.[81]

---

[81] Congress's response to *Citizen Publishing* further convinces us that we should not carve out an exception to the Sherman Act simply because the type of venture at issue here may be economically efficient. Shortly after the decision, Congress passed the Newspaper Preservation Act, 15 U.S.C. §§ 801-1804, which specifically exempted from the Sherman Act newspaper operating arrangements like the one in *Citizen Publishing*. *See Hawaii Newspaper Agency v. Bronster*, 103 F.3d 742, 744-45 (9th Cir. 1996). After surveying the relevant "economic conditions," Congress determined that the specific type of joint venture at issue was beneficial and even necessary in a "large majority of American communities." H.R. Rep. No. 91-1193, 91st Cong., 2d Sess. (1970), *reprinted in* 1970 U.S.C.C.A.N. 3547, 3548. Those economic conditions, in Congress's view, justified more lenient antitrust review of newspaper industry

Footnote continued on next page

We therefore hold that the district court erred in finding no triable issue of fact with respect to the plaintiffs' *per se* claim. The plaintiffs have presented sufficient evidence to create a triable issue of fact as to whether the alliance's unified pricing scheme was a *per se* violation of § 1 of the Sherman Act.

CONCLUSION

For the reasons stated above, we AFFIRM the district court's award of summary judgment to defendant Saudi Refining, Inc., REVERSE the district court's award of summary judgment against the Plaintiffs Appellants, and REMAND for further proceedings consistent with this opinion.

FERNANDEZ, Circuit Judge, Concurring and Dissenting:

I agree that the plaintiffs lacked standing as to SRI and, therefore, concur in the result of part III of the majority opinion. However, I dissent from part IV.

While this case does involve a very complicated set of transactions, it presents a rather straightforward antitrust law question. That is, where former competitors create a bona fide joint venture to which all of their assets and operations in segments of their businesses are contributed, will there be a *per se* violation of the antitrust laws, if the joint venture entity sets the prices of the goods it sells? I think the answer is no.

Here, Shell and Texaco formed Equilon Enterprises, LLC in the western United States, and Motiva Enterprises, LLC in the eastern

---

Footnote continued from previous page

joint ventures than the Court had applied in *Citizen Publishing*. Congress has made no such findings, nor has it passed any similar law, relevant to the oil and gasoline industry, which certainly is not without its supporters in the Legislative and Executive Branch. If Congress wishes to exempt oil and gasoline enterprises from the Sherman Act's *per se* prohibition of price fixing, it may certainly do so, but it is beyond our authority to read new exceptions into the Act.

United States.[82] There can be no doubt that each of the new entities is a true, bona fide, economically integrated joint venture. Refineries, lubricant plants, research laboratories, thousands of service stations, thousands of miles of pipeline, thousands of employees, and over 100 terminals were contributed to the ventures. Upon those transfers, Shell and Texaco ceased refining and marketing operations in both the western and the eastern United States. They were no longer in those businesses within the United States; the joint ventures were.[83] In other words, Equilon now manufactured, inventoried, transported, and marketed the products. It ran the refinery; it had the research facilities; it transported products: and it dealt with the station operators and other buyers. It also priced the products, and set the same price for its Shell and Texaco brands.

While Independent Operators do not assert that the placing of the whole manufacturing, transport and marketing functions in a single entity violated 15 U.S.C. § 1, they do assert that having the pricing function in Equilon did violate the antitrust laws *per se*. The majority thinks that might be true; I do not.

It is plain enough that the mere creation of a joint venture is not a *per se* antitrust violation. No doubt, like mergers, joint ventures are combinations of business assets but "such combinations are judged under a rule of reason" analysis. *Copperweld Corp. v. Independence Tube Corp.*, 467 U.S. 752, 768, 104 S. Ct. 2731, 2740, 81 L.Ed.2d 628 (1984). Especially should that be true of the LLC type of venture, which is not only a separate entity, but which also

---

[82]   Henceforth, I shall only refer to Equilon because it is the entity that directly affects plaintiffs in this case-Independent Operators.

[83]   We have previously had occasion to describe the nature of Equilon. *See Abrahim & Sons Enters. v. Equilon Enters., LLC*, 292 F.3d 958, 960 (9th Cir. 2002). As we stated, an LLC is an entity truly distinct from its members and its acts "are deemed independent of the acts of its members." *Id.* at 962. It is a separate juridical person. *Id.* LLCs are much like corporations, and, though controlled by their members," LLCs remain separate and distinct from their members." *Id.*

functions as a separate economic unit for all practical purposes. *See Northrop Corp. v. McDonnell Douglas Corp.*, 705 F.2d 1030, 1053 (9th Cir. 1983). In fact, to slightly paraphrase the Supreme Court statement in *Arizona v. Maricopa County Med. Soc'y*, 457 U.S. 332, 356, 102 S. Ct. 2466, 2479, 73 L.Ed.2d 48 (1982):

> [Equilon is] . . . analogous to partnerships or other joint arrangements in which persons who would otherwise be competitors pool their capital and share the risks of loss as well as the opportunities for profit. In such joint ventures, the partnership is regarded as a single firm competing with other sellers in the market.

Nor does the mere fact that Equilon sets prices for the products it manufactures and sells suffice to demonstrate that its actions were price fixing for antitrust purposes. *See Broad. Music, Inc. v. Columbia Broad. Sys., Inc.*, 441 1, 8-9, 99 S. Ct. 1551, 1556-57, 60 L.Ed.2d 1 (1979). Rather, "[l]iteralness is overly simplistic and often overbroad. When two partners set the price of their goods or services they are literally 'price fixing,' but they are not *per se* in violation of the Sherman Act." So just what could make the operation of Equilon a *per se* violation of the antitrust laws? Surely it is not a claim that the venture is a sham. *See Addamax Corp. v. Open Software Found., Inc.*, 152 F.3d 48, 52 (1st Cir. 1998). No one seriously asserts *that*.

Nor can it be that this is a case like *Citizen Publ'g Co. v. United States*, 394 U.S. 131, 89 S. Ct. 927, 22 L.Ed.2d 148 (1969). There, two newspapers formed a third corporation for the principal purpose of eliminating competition, but each remained in the same business in the same area, and retained the production of the true product - news and editorials -- in its own hands. *Id.* at 133, 89 S. Ct. at 928. Moreover, the newspapers themselves - not the new entity - jointly set the subscription and advertising rates. *Id.* at 134, 89 S. Ct. at 928. None of that is true here. Equilon owned all of the assets, all of the obligations, and, in a word, the whole business. It set the prices. It was a separate entity; a fact that the Independent Operators seem unable or unwilling to grasp.

But, Independent Operators argue, in this case the fixing of prices by the venture is neither essential nor "reasonably ancillary to the legitimate cooperative aspects of the venture." *Freeman v. San Diego Ass'n of Realtors*, 322 F.3d 1133, 1151 (9th Cir. 2003). The majority agrees; I cannot understand why. The situation here is far from the kind of situation we faced in *Freeman*. There, the reason for the venture was the unifying of disparate multiple listing databases. *Id.* at 1140-41. That done, there was a new database entity, and the corporations that formed it for that purpose went on operating their own businesses. But they all also agreed to fix a price for support services. That was essentially unrelated to the database itself, and was unnecessary, and unjustified. *Id.* at 1151. It was the latter "price fix" that ran afoul of antitrust principles. Here we have nothing of the kind.

In this case, nothing more radical is afoot than the fact that an entity, which now owns all of the production, transportation, research, storage, sales and distribution facilities for engaging in the gasoline business, also prices its own products. It decided to price them the same, as any other entity could. What could be more integral to the running of a business than setting a price for its goods and services? I am at a loss for an answer to that question, and nothing written about this case to date imparts additional wisdom or better information.

Yet Independent Operators insist that the setting of the prices is a violation. That is, separate juridical business entity though it is, Equilon can really only be the semblance of a true business, for if it, like any other economic actor, desires to price its own goods, its members may well be subject not merely to commination, but to outright denunciation by the courts as *per se* violators of the antitrust laws. It means that this entity must ask a separate juridical entity -- for example, Shell, which does not itself own any of the facilities or products-to decide what price should be charged by Equilon.[84] Again, the majority thinks that might be so; I do not.

We now have an exotic beast, no less strange than a manticore, roaming the business world. This beast would otherwise be a true business, but when it acts like a true business -- sets prices for its own goods -- it subjects its otherwise insulated members to the severe sting of antitrust liability. While it has the head of a business man and the body of an entrepreneurial lion, it has the tail of a liability scorpion. I suppose I am as taken with stories of exotic beasts as the next person, but I prefer to leave them in the realm of the unknown; I would rather not confront them in the marketplace.

In short, I do not believe that the Independent Operators have pointed to a *per se* antitrust violation,[85] and they do not even attempt to assert a full rule of reason claim.

Thus, I respectfully dissent as to part IV of the majority opinion.

NOTE

Certiorari has been granted and this case is scheduled to be reviewed by the Supreme Court in the 2005-06 term of the Court.

---

[84] Shell, by the way, is a mere member of Equilon and is shielded from liability for the debts or obligations of Equilon, just as corporate shareholders are shielded. *See* Cal. Corp. Code § 17101.

[85] Similarly, no "quick look" violation is shown. *See* Cal. Dental Ass'n v. FTC, 526 U.S. 756, 770, 119 S. Ct. 1604, 1612, 143 L.Ed.2d 935 (1999); Bogan v. Hodgkins, 166 F.3d 509, 514 n. 6 (2d Cir. 1999).

CHAPTER 11: FOREIGN COMMERCE AND THE U.S. ANTITRUST LAWS

Insert as replacement to pages 1216-1229.

F. HOFFMANN-LA ROCHE v. *EMPAGRAN*

Supreme Court of the United States, 2004

542 U.S. 155, 124 S.CT. 2359, 159 L. ED. 2D 226

BREYER, J The Foreign Trade Antitrust Improvements Act of 1982 (FTAIA) excludes from the Sherman Act's reach much anticompetitive conduct that causes only foreign injury. It does so by setting forth a general rule stating that the Sherman Act "shall not apply to conduct involving trade or commerce . . . with foreign nations." It then creates exceptions to the general rule, applicable where (roughly speaking) that conduct significantly harms imports, domestic commerce, or American exporters.

We here focus upon anticompetitive price-fixing activity that is in significant part foreign, that causes some domestic antitrust injury, and that independently causes separate foreign injury. We ask two questions about the price-fixing conduct and the foreign injury that it causes. First, does that conduct fall within the FTAIA's general rule excluding the Sherman Act's application? That is to say, does the price-fixing activity constitute "conduct involving trade or commerce . . . with foreign nations"? We conclude that it does.

Second, we ask whether the conduct nonetheless falls within a domestic-injury exception to the general rule, an exception that applies (and makes the Sherman Act nonetheless applicable) where the conduct (1) has a "direct, substantial, and reasonably foreseeable effect" on domestic commerce, and (2) "such effect gives rise to a [Sherman Act] claim." §§a(1)(A), (2). We conclude that the exception does not apply where the plaintiff's claim rests solely on the independent foreign harm.

To clarify: The issue before us concerns (1) significant foreign anticompetitive conduct with (2) an adverse domestic effect and (3) an independent foreign effect giving rise to the claim. In

115

more concrete terms, this case involves vitamin sellers around the world that agreed to fix prices, leading to higher vitamin prices in the United States and independently leading to higher vitamin prices in other countries such as Ecuador. We conclude that, in this scenario, a purchaser in the United States could bring a Sherman Act claim under FTAIA based on domestic injury, but a purchaser in Ecuador could not bring a Sherman Act claim based on foreign harm.

The plaintiffs in this case originally filed a class-action suit on behalf of foreign and domestic purchasers of vitamins under, *inter alia*, §1 of the Sherman Act, 26 Stat. 209, as amended, 15 U.S.C. §1 and §4 and 16 of the Clayton Act, 28 Stat. 731, 737, as amended, 15 U.S.C. §§15-26. Their complaint alleged that petitioners, foreign and domestic vitamin manufacturers and distributors, had engaged in a price-fixing conspiracy, raising the price of vitamin products to customers in the United States and to customers in foreign countries.

As relevant there, petitioners moved to dismiss the suit as to the *foreign* purchasers (the respondents here), five foreign vitamin distributors located in Ukraine, Australia, Ecuador, and Panama, each of which bought vitamins from petitioners for delivery outside the United States describing the relevant transactions as "wholly foreign"). Respondents have never asserted that they purchased any vitamins in the United States or in transactions in United States commerce, and the question presented assumes that the relevant "transactions occurr[ed] entirely outside U.S. commerce." The District Court dismissed their claims. *Ibid.* It applied the FTAIA and found none of the exceptions applicable. *Id.*, at *3-*4. Thereafter, the domestic purchasers transferred their claims to another pending suit and did not take part in the subsequent appeal.

A divided panel of the Court of Appeals reversed. 315 F. 3d 338. The panel concluded that the FTAJA's general exclusionary rule applied to the case, but that its domestic-injury exception also applied. It basically read the plaintiffs' complaint to allege that the vitamin manufacturers' price-fixing conspiracy (1) had "a direct, substantial, and reasonably foreseeable effect" on ordinary domestic trade or commerce, i.e., the conspiracy brought about higher domestic vitamin prices, and (2) "such effect" gave "rise to a [Sherman Act] claim," i.e., an injured domestic customer could have brought a Sherman Act

116

suit, 15 U.S.C. §§6a(1), (2). Those allegations, the court held, are sufficient to meet the exception's requirements. 315 F. 3d, at 341.

The court assumed that the foreign effect, i.e., higher prices in Ukraine, Panama, Australia, and Ecuador, was independent of the domestic effect, i.e., higher domestic prices. Ibid. But it concluded that, in light of the FTAIA's text, legislative history, and the policy goal of deterring harmful price-fixing activity, this lack of connection does not matter. Ibid. The District of Columbia Circuit denied rehearing *en banc* by a 4-to-3 vote.

We granted certiorari to resolve a split among the Courts of Appeals about the exception's application. Compare *Den Norske Stats Oljeselskap As* v. *HeereMac Vof,* 241 F. 3d 420, 427 (CA5 2001) (exception does not apply where foreign injury independent of domestic harm), with *Kruman* v. *Christie's Int'l PLC,* 284 F. 3d 384, 400 (CA2 2002) (exception does apply even where foreign injury independent); 315 F. 3d, at 341 (similar).

The FTAIA seeks to make clear to American exporters (and to firms doing business abroad) that the Sherman Act does not prevent them from entering into business arrangements (say, joint-selling arrangements), however anticompetitive, as long as those arrangements adversely affect only foreign markets. See H. R. Rep. No. 97-686, pp. 1-3, 9-10 (1982) (hereinafter House Report). It does so by removing from the Sherman Act's reach, (1) export activities and (2) other commercial activities taking place abroad, unless those activities adversely affect domestic commerce, imports to the United States, or exporting activities of one engaged in such activities within the United States.

The FTAIA says:

> "Sections 1 to 7 of this title [the Sherman Act] shall not apply to conduct involving trade or commerce (other than import trade or import commerce) with foreign nations unless—

"(1) such conduct has a direct, substantial, and reasonably foreseeable effect — "

(A) on trade or commerce which is not trade or commerce with foreign nations [i.e., domestic trade or commerce], or on import trade or import commerce with foreign nations; or

"(B) on export trade or export commerce with foreign nations, of a person engaged in such trade or commerce in the United States [i.e., on an American export competitor]; and

(2)   such effect gives rise to a claim under the provisions of sections 1 to 7 of this title, other than this section.

"If sections 1 to 7 of this title apply to such conduct only because of the operation of paragraph (1)(B), then sections 1 to 7 of this title shall apply to such conduct only for injury to export business in the United States."   15 U.S.C. §6a.

This technical language initially lays down a general rule placing *all* (non-import) activity involving foreign commerce outside the Sherman Act's reach. It then brings such conduct back within the Sherman Act's reach *provided that* the conduct *both* (1) sufficiently affects American commerce, i.e., it has a "direct, substantial, and reasonably foreseeable effect" on American domestic, import, or (certain) export commerce, and (2) has an effect of a kind that antitrust law considers harmful, i.e., the "effect" must "giv[e] rise to a [Sherman Act] claim." §§6a(1), (2).

We ask here how this language applies to price-fixing activity that is in significant part foreign, that has the requisite domestic effect, and that also has independent foreign effects giving rise to the plaintiffs claim.

Respondents make a threshold argument. They say that the transactions here at issue fall outside the FTAIA because the FTAIA's general exclusionary rule applies only to conduct involving exports. The rule says that the Sherman Act "shall not apply to conduct involving trade or commerce (other than import trade or import commerce) *with* foreign nations." §6a (emphasis added). The word "with" means *between* the United States and foreign nations. And, they contend, commerce between the United States and foreign nations that is not import commerce must consist of export commerce - a kind of commerce irrelevant to the case at hand.

The difficulty with respondents' argument is that the FTAIA originated in a bill that initially referred only to "export trade or export commerce." H.R. 5235, 97th Cong., 1st Sess., §1 (1981). But the House Judiciary Committee subsequently changed that language to "trade or commerce (other than import trade or import commerce)." 15 U.S.C. §6a. And it did so deliberately to include commerce that did not involve American exports but which was wholly foreign.

The House Report says in relevant part:

> "The Subcommittee's 'export' commerce limitation appeared to make the amendments inapplicable to transactions that were neither import nor export, i.e., transactions within, between, or among other nations. . . Such foreign transactions should, for the purposes of this legislation, be treated in the same manner as export transactions - that is, there should be no American antitrust jurisdiction absent a direct, substantial and reasonably foreseeable effect on domestic commerce or a domestic competitor. The Committee Amendment therefore deletes references to 'export' trade, and

119

substitutes phrases such as 'other than import' trade. It is thus clear that wholly foreign transactions as well as export transactions are covered by the amendment, but that import transactions are not." House Report 9-10 (emphases added).

For those who find legislative history useful, the House Report's account should end the matter. Others, by considering carefully the amendment itself and the lack of any other plausible purpose, may reach the same conclusion, namely that the FTAIA's general rule applies where the anticompetitive conduct at issue is foreign.

We turn now to the basic question presented, that of the exception's application. Because the underlying antitrust action is complex, potentially raising questions not directly at issue here, we reemphasize that we base our decision upon the following: The price-fixing conduct significantly and adversely affects both customers outside the United States and customers within the United States, but the adverse foreign effect is independent of any adverse domestic effect. In these circumstances, we find that the FTAIA exception does not apply (and thus the Sherman Act does not apply) for two main reasons.

First, this Court ordinarily construes ambiguous statutes to avoid unreasonable interference with the sovereign authority of other nations. See, *e.g., McCulloch* v. *Sociedad Nacional de Marineros de Honduras*, 372 U.S. 10, 20-22 (1963) (application of National Labor Relations Act to foreign-flag vessels); *Romero* v. *International Terminal Operating Co.*, 358 U.S. 354, 382-383 (1959) (application of Jones Act in maritime case); *Lauritzen v. Larsen*, 345 U.S. 571, 578 (1953) (same). This rule of construction reflects principles of customary international law - law that (we must assume) Congress ordinarily seeks to follow. See Restatement (Third) of Foreign Relations Law of the United States §§403(1), 403(2) (1986) (hereinafter Restatement) (limiting the unreasonable exercise of prescriptive jurisdiction with respect to a person or activity having connections with another State); *Murray* v. *Schooner Charming*

120

Betsy, 2 Cranch 64, 118 (1804) ("[A]n act of Congress ought never to be construed to violate the law of nations if any other possible construction remains"); *Hartford Fire Insurance Co.* v. *California*, 509 U.S. 764, 817 (1993) (SCALIA, J., dissenting) (identifying rule of construction as derived from the principle of "prescriptive comity").

This rule of statutory construction cautions courts to assume that legislators take account of the legitimate sovereign interests of other nations when they write American laws. It thereby helps the potentially conflicting laws of different nations work together in harmony - a harmony particularly needed in today's highly interdependent commercial world.

No one denies that America's antitrust laws, when applied to foreign conduct, can interfere with a foreign nation's ability independently to regulate its own commercial affairs. But our courts have long held that application of our antitrust laws to foreign anticompetitive conduct is nonetheless reasonable, and hence consistent with principles of prescriptive comity, insofar as they reflect a legislative effort to redress domestic antitrust injury that foreign anticompetitive conduct has caused. See *United States* v. *Aluminum Co. of America*, 148 F. 2d 416, 443-444 (CA2 1945) (L. Hand, J.); 1 P. Areeda & D. Turner, Antitrust Law ¶236 (1978).

But why is it reasonable to apply those laws to foreign conduct *insofar as that conduct causes independent foreign harm and that foreign harm alone gives rise to the plaintiff's claim?* Like the former case, application of those laws creates a serious risk of interference with a foreign nation's ability independently to regulate its own commercial affairs. But, unlike the former case, the justification for that interference seems insubstantial. See Restatement §403(2) (determining reasonableness on basis of such factors as connections with regulating nation, harm to that nation's interests, extent to which other nations regulate, and the potential for conflict). Why should American law supplant, for example, Canada's or Great Britain's or Japan's own determination about how best to protect Canadian or British or Japanese customers from anticompetitive conduct engaged in significant part by Canadian or British or Japanese or other foreign companies?

121

We recognize that principles of comity provide Congress greater leeway when it seeks to control through legislation the actions of *American* companies, see Restatement §402; and some of the anticompetitive price-fixing conduct alleged here took place in *America*. But the higher foreign prices of which the foreign plaintiffs here complain are not the consequence of any domestic anticompetitive conduct *that Congress sought to forbid*, for Congress did not seek to forbid any such conduct insofar as it is here relevant, i.e., insofar as it is intertwined with foreign conduct that causes independent foreign harm. Rather Congress sought to release domestic (and foreign) anticompetitive conduct from Sherman Act constraints when that conduct causes foreign harm. Congress, of course, did make an exception where that conduct also causes domestic harm. See House Report 13 (concerns about American firms' participation in international cartels addressed through "domestic injury" exception). But any independent domestic harm the foreign conduct causes here has, by definition, little or nothing to do with the matter.

We thus repeat the basic question: Why is it reasonable to apply this law to conduct that is significantly foreign *insofar as that conduct causes independent foreign harm and that foreign harm alone gives rise to the plaintiff's claim?* We can find no good answer to the question.

The Areeda and Hovenkamp treatise notes that under the Court of Appeals' interpretation of the statute

> "a Malaysian customer could . . . maintain an action under United States law in a United States court against its own Malaysian supplier, another cartel member, simply by noting that unnamed third parties injured [in the United States] by the American [cartel member's] conduct would also have a cause of action.

> Effectively, the United States courts would provide worldwide subject

122

matter jurisdiction to any foreign suitor wishing to sue its own local supplier, but unhappy with its own sovereign's provisions for private antitrust enforcement, provided that a different plaintiff had a cause of action against a different firm for injuries that were within U.S. [other-than-import] commerce. It does not seem excessively rigid to infer that Congress would not have intended that result." P. Areeda & H. Hovenkamp, Antitrust Law ¶273, pp. 51-52 (Supp. 2003).

We agree with the comment. We can find no convincing justification for the extension of the Sherman Act's scope that it describes.

Respondents reply that many nations have adopted antitrust laws similar to our own, to the point where the practical likelihood of interference with the relevant interests of other nations is minimal. Leaving price fixing to the side, however, this Court has found to the contrary. See, e.g., *Hartford Fire*, 509 U.S. at 797-799 (noting that the alleged conduct in the London reinsurance market, while illegal under United States antitrust laws, was assumed to be perfectly consistent with British law and policy); see also, *e.g.,* 2 W. Fugate, Foreign Commerce and the Antitrust Laws §16.6 (5th ed. 1996) (noting differences between European Union and United States law on vertical restraints).

Regardless, even where nations agree about primary conduct, say price fixing, they disagree dramatically about appropriate remedies. The application, for example, of American private treble-damages remedies to anticompetitive conduct taking place abroad has generated considerable controversy. See, *e.g.*, 2 ABA Section of Antitrust Law, Antitrust Law Developments 1208-1209 (5th ed. 2002). And several foreign nations have filed briefs here arguing that to apply our remedies would unjustifiably permit their citizens to bypass their own less generous remedial schemes, thereby upsetting a balance of competing considerations that their own domestic antitrust laws embody. *E.g.*, Brief for Federal Republic of Germany et al. as *Amici Curiae* 2 (setting forth German interest "in seeing that German companies are not subject to the extraterritorial reach of the United States' antitrust laws by private foreign plaintiffs - whose injuries were sustained in transactions entirely outside United States commerce - seeking treble damages in private lawsuits against German companies"); Brief for Government of Canada as *Amicus Curiae* 14 ("treble damages remedy would supersede" Canada's "national policy decision"); Brief for Government of Japan as *Amicus Curiae* 10 (finding "particularly troublesome" the potential "interfere[nce] with Japanese governmental regulation of the Japanese market").

These briefs add that a decision permitting independently injured foreign plaintiffs to pursue private treble-damages remedies would undermine foreign nations' own antitrust enforcement policies by diminishing foreign firms' incentive to cooperate with antitrust authorities in return for prosecutorial amnesty. Brief for Federal Republic of Germany et al. as *Amici Curiae* 28-30; Brief for Government of Canada as *Amicus Curiae* 11-14. See also Brief for United States as *Amicus Curiae* 19-21 (arguing the same in respect to American antitrust enforcement).

Respondents alternatively argue that comity does not demand an interpretation of the FTAIA that would exclude independent foreign injury cases across the board. Rather, courts can take (and sometimes have taken) account of comity considerations case by case, abstaining where comity considerations so dictate. Cf., *e.g., Hartford Fire, supra*, at 797, n. 24; *United States* v. *Nippon Paper Industries Co.*, 109 F. 3d 1, 8 (CA1 1997); *Mannington Mills, Inc.* v. *Congoleum Corp.*, 595 F. 2d 1287, 1294-1295 (CA3 1979).

In our view, however, this approach is too complex to prove workable. The Sherman Act covers many different kinds of anticompetitive agreements. Courts would have to examine how foreign law, compared with American law, treats not only price fixing but also, say, information-sharing agreements, patent-licensing price conditions, territorial product resale limitations, and various forms of joint venture, in respect to both primary conduct and remedy. The legally and economically technical nature of that enterprise means lengthier proceedings, appeals, and more proceedings - to the point where procedural costs and delays could themselves threaten interference with a foreign nation's ability to maintain the integrity of its own antitrust enforcement system. Even in this relatively simple price-fixing case, for example, competing briefs tell us (1) that potential treble-damage liability would help enforce widespread anti-price-fixing norms (through added deterrence) and (2) the opposite, namely that such liability would hinder antitrust enforcement (by reducing incentives to enter amnesty programs). Compare, *e.g.*, Brief for Certain Professors of Economics as *Amici Curiae* 2-4 with Brief for United States as *Amicus Curiae* 19-21. How could a court seriously interested in resolving so empirical a matter - a matter potentially related to impact on foreign interests - do so simply and expeditiously?

We conclude that principles of prescriptive comity counsel against the Court of Appeals' interpretation of the FTAIA. Where foreign anticompetitive conduct plays a significant role and where foreign injury is independent of domestic effects, Congress might have hoped that America's antitrust laws, so fundamental a component of our own economic system, would commend themselves to other nations as well. But, if America's antitrust policies could not win their own way in the international marketplace for such ideas, Congress, we must assume, would not have tried to impose them, in an act of legal imperialism, through legislative fiat.

Second, the FTAIA's language and history suggest that Congress designed the FTAIA to clarify, perhaps to limit, but not to *expand* in any significant way, the Sherman Act's scope as applied, to foreign commerce. See House Report 2-3. And we have found no significant indication that at the time Congress wrote this statute courts would have thought the Sherman Act applicable in these circumstances.

The Solicitor General and petitioners tell us that they have found no case in which any court applied the Sherman Act to redress foreign injury in such circumstances. Tr. of Oral Arg. 21; Brief for United States as *Amicus Curiae* 13; Brief for Petitioners 13; see also *Den Norske*, 241 F. 3d, at 429 ("[W]e have found no case in which jurisdiction was found in a case like this - where a foreign plaintiff is injured in a foreign market with no injuries arising from the anticompetitive effect on a United States market"). And respondents themselves apparently conceded as much at a May 23, 2001, hearing before the District Court below. 2001 WL 761360, at *4.

Nevertheless, respondents now have called to our attention six cases, three decided by this Court and three decided by lower courts. In the first three cases the defendants included both American companies and foreign companies jointly engaged in anticompetitive behavior having both foreign and domestic effects. See *Timken Roller Bearing Co.* v. *United States*, 341 U.S. 593, 595 (1951) (agreements among American, British, and French corporations to eliminate competition in the manufacture and sale of anti-friction bearings in world, including United States, markets); *United States* v. *National Lead Co.*, 332 U.S. 319, 325-328 (1947) (international cartels with American and foreign members, restraining international commerce, including United States commerce, in titanium pigments); *United States* v. *American Tobacco Co.*, 221 U.S. 106, 171-172 (1911) (American tobacco corporations agreed in England with British company to divide world markets). In all three cases the plaintiff sought relief, including relief that might have helped to protect those injured abroad.

In all three cases, however, the plaintiff was the Government of the United States. A Government plaintiff, unlike a private plaintiff, must seek to obtain the relief necessary to protect the public from further anticompetitive conduct and to redress anticompetitive harm. And a Government plaintiff has legal authority broad enough to allow it to carry out this mission. 15 U.S.C. §25; see also, *e.g., United States* v. *E. I. du Pont de Nemours & Co.*, 366 U.S. 316, 334 (1961) ("[I]t is well settled that once the Government has successfully borne the considerable burden of establishing a violation of law, all doubts as to the remedy are to be resolved in its favor"). Private plaintiffs, by way of contrast, are far less likely to be able to secure broad relief. See *California* v. *American Stores Co.*, 495 U.S. 271, 295 (1990) ("Our conclusion that a district court has the power to order divestiture in appropriate cases brought [by private plaintiffs] does not, of course, mean that such power should be exercised in every situation in which the Government would be entitled to such relief"); 2 P. Areeda & H. Hovenkamp, Antitrust Law §§303d-303e, pp. 40-45 (2d ed. 2000) (distinguishing between private and government suits in terms of availability, public interest motives, and remedial scope); Griffin, Extraterritoriality in U.S. and EU Antitrust Enforcement, 67 Antitrust L. J. 159, 194 (1999) ("[P]rivate plaintiffs often are unwilling to exercise the degree of self-restraint and consideration of foreign governmental sensibilities generally exercised by the U.S. Government"). This difference means that the Government's ability, in these three cases, to obtain relief helpful to those injured abroad tells us little or nothing about whether this Court would have awarded similar relief at the request of private plaintiffs.

Neither did the Court focus explicitly in its opinions on a claim that the remedies sought to cure only independently caused foreign harm. Thus the three cases tell us even less about whether this Court then thought that foreign private plaintiffs could have obtained foreign relief based solely upon such independently caused foreign injury.

Respondents also refer to three lower court cases brought by private plaintiffs. In the first, *Industria Siciliana Asfalti, Bitumi, S. p. A. v. Exxon Research & Engineering Co.*, 1977 WL 1353 (SDNY, Jan. 18, 1977), a District Court permitted an Italian firm to proceed against an American firm with a Sherman Act claim based upon a purely foreign injury, *i.e.*, an injury suffered in Italy. The court made clear, however, that the foreign injury was *"inextricably bound up with . . . domestic restraints of trade,"* and that the plaintiff *"was injured . . . by reason of an alleged restraint of our domestic trade,"* *id.*, at *11, *12 (emphasis added), *i.e.*, the foreign injury was dependent upon, *not independent of*, domestic harm. See Part VI, infra.

In the second case, *Dominicus Americana Bohio v. Gulf & Western Industries, Inc.*, 473 F. Supp. 680 (SDNY 1979), a District Court permitted Dominican and American firms to proceed against a competing American firm and the Dominican Tourist Information Center with a Sherman Act claim based upon injury apparently suffered in the Dominican Republic. The court, in finding the Sherman Act applicable, weighed several different factors, including the participation of American firms in the unlawful conduct, the partly domestic nature of both conduct and harm (to American tourists, a kind of "export"), and the fact that the domestic harm depended in part upon the foreign injury. *Id.*, at 688. The court did not separately analyze the legal problem before it in terms of independently caused foreign injury. Its opinion simply does not discuss the matter. It consequently cannot be taken as significant support for application of the Sherman Act here.

The third case, *Hunt* v. *Mobil Oil Corp.*, 550 F. 2d 68, 72 (CA2 1977), involved a claim by Hunt, an independent oil producer with reserves in Libya, that other major oil producers in Libya and the Persian Gulf (the "seven majors") had conspired in New York and elsewhere to make it more difficult for Hunt to reach agreement with the Libyan government on production terms and thereby eliminate him as a competitor. The case can be seen as involving a primarily foreign conspiracy designed to bring about foreign injury in Libya. But, as in *Dominicus*, the court nowhere considered the problem of independently caused foreign harm. Rather, the case was about the "act of state" doctrine, and the sole discussion of Sherman Act applicability – one brief paragraph - refers to other matters. 550 F. 2d, at 72, and n. 2. We do not see how Congress could have taken this case as significant support for the proposition that the Sherman Act applies in present circumstances.

The upshot is that no pre-1982 case provides significant authority for application of the Sherman Act in the circumstances we here assume. Indeed, a leading contemporaneous lower court case contains language suggesting the contrary. See *Timberlane Lumber Co.* v. *Bank of America*, 549 F. 2d 597, 613 (CA9 1976) (insisting that the foreign conduct's domestic effect be "sufficiently large to present a cognizable injury to the plaintiffs" (emphasis added)).

Taken together, these two sets of considerations, the one derived from comity and the other reflecting history, convince us that Congress would not have intended the FTAIA's exception to bring independently caused foreign injury within the Sherman Act's reach.

V

Respondents point to several considerations that point the other way. For one thing, the FTAIA's language speaks in terms of

128

the Sherman Act's *applicability* to certain kinds of *conduct*. The FTAIA says that the Sherman Act applies to foreign "conduct" with a certain kind of harmful domestic effect. Why isn't that the end of the matter? How can the Sherman Act both *apply to the conduct* when one person sues but *not apply to the same conduct* when another person sues? The question of who can or cannot sue is a matter for other statutes (namely, the Clayton Act) to determine.

Moreover, the exception says that it applies if the conduct's domestic effect gives rise to "a claim," not to *"the plaintiff's claim"* or *"the claim at issue."* 15 U.S.C. §6a(2) (emphasis added). The alleged conduct here did have domestic effects, and those effects were harmful enough to give rise to "a" claim. Respondents concede that this claim is not their own claim; it is someone else's claim. But, linguistically speaking, they say, that is beside the point. Nor did Congress place the relevant words "gives rise to a claim" in the FTAIA to suggest any geographical limitation; rather it did so for a more neutral reason, namely, in order to make clear that the domestic effect must be an adverse (as opposed to a beneficial) effect. See House Report 11 (citing *National Bank of Canada* v. *Interbank Card Assn.*, 666 F. 2d 6, 8 (CA2 1981)).

Despite their linguistic logic, these arguments are not convincing. Linguistically speaking, a statute can apply and not apply to the same conduct, depending upon other circumstances; and those other circumstances may include the nature of the lawsuit (or of the related underlying harm). It also makes linguistic sense to read the words "a claim" as if they refer to the "plaintiffs claim" or "the claim at issue."

At most, respondents' linguistic arguments might show that respondents' reading is the more natural reading of the statutory language. But those arguments do not show that we *must* accept that reading. And that is the critical point. The considerations previously mentioned - those of comity and history - make clear that the respondents' reading is not consistent with the FTAIA's basic intent. If the statute's language reasonably permits an interpretation consistent with that intent, we should adopt it. And, for the reasons stated, we believe that the statute's language permits the reading that we give it.

Finally, respondents point to policy considerations that we have previously discussed, *supra*, at 11, namely, that application of the Sherman Act in present circumstances will (through increased deterrence) help protect Americans against foreign-caused anticompetitive injury. As we have explained, however, the plaintiffs and supporting enforcement-agency *amici* have made important experience-backed arguments (based upon amnesty-seeking incentives) to the contrary. We cannot say whether, on balance, respondents' side of this empirically based argument or the enforcement agencies' side is correct. But we can say that the answer to the dispute is neither clear enough, nor of such likely empirical significance, that it could overcome the considerations we have previously discussed and change our conclusion.

For these reasons, we conclude that petitioners' reading of the statute's language is correct. That reading furthers the statute's basic purposes, it properly reflects considerations of comity, and it is consistent with Sherman Act history.

VI

We have assumed that the anticompetitive conduct here independently caused foreign injury; that is, the conduct's domestic effects did not help to bring about that foreign injury. Respondents argue, in the alternative, that the foreign injury was not independent. Rather, they say, the anticompetitive conduct's domestic effects were linked to that foreign harm. Respondents contend that, because vitamins are fungible and readily transportable, without an adverse domestic effect (*i.e.*, higher prices in the United States), the sellers could not have maintained their international price-fixing arrangement and respondents would not have suffered their foreign injury. They add that this "but for" condition is sufficient to bring the price-fixing conduct within the scope of the FTAIA's exception.

The Court of Appeals, however, did not address this argument, 315 F. 3d, at 341, and, for that reason, neither shall we. Respondents remain free to ask the Court of Appeals to consider the claim. The Court of Appeals may determine whether respondents properly preserved the argument, and, if so, it may consider it and decide the related claim.

130

For these reasons, the judgment of the Court of Appeals is vacated, and the case is remanded for further proceedings consistent with this opinion.

O'CONNOR, J. took no part in the consideration or decision of this case.

SCALIA, J. with whom JUSTICE THOMAS J. concurring in the judgment.

I concur in the judgment of the Court because the language of the statute is readily susceptible of the interpretation the Court provides and because only that interpretation is consistent with the principle that statutes should be read in accord with the customary deference to the application of foreign countries' laws within their own territories.

Insert after Supreme Court's *Empagran* decision, page 1231

EMPAGRAN SA, et al. v. *F.HOFFMANN-LAROCHE, LTD, et al*

United States Court of Appeals, DC Circuit, 2005

___F.3rd___

HENDERSON, J.   The appellants, foreign corporations that purchased vitamin products outside of the United States for distribution in foreign countries from the appellee foreign manufacturers, brought this action asserting, *inter alia,* price fixing in violation of the Sherman Act.   The district court dismissed the Sherman Act claim for lack of subject matter jurisdiction under the Foreign Trade Antitrust Improvements Act (FTAIA), which makes the Sherman Act inapplicable to conduct involving non-import foreign trade or commerce with one exception: when "such conduct has a direct, substantial, and reasonably foreseeable effect" on *domestic* trade or commerce and "such effect gives rise to a claim under [the Sherman Act].   This court in a divided opinion reversed the district court, reasoning that "where the anticompetitive conduct has the requisite harm on United States commerce, FTAIA permits suits by foreign plaintiffs who are injured solely by that conduct's effect on foreign commerce."   The United States Supreme Court granted *certiorari* and vacated this court's decision concluding that under the FTAIA the Sherman Act does not apply where "price-fixing conduct significantly and adversely affects both customers outside the United States and customers within the United States, but the adverse foreign effect is independent of any adverse domestic effect." *F. Hoffman-La Roche, Ltd. v. Empagran S.A.,* 124 S.Ct. 2359, 2366 (2004).   The Supreme Court remanded to this court, however, to assess the appellants' alternate theory for Sherman Act liability, namely, that "because vitamins are fungible and readily transportable, without an adverse domestic effect (*i.e.,* higher prices in the United States), the sellers could not have maintained their international price-fixing arrangement and respondents would not have suffered their foreign injury." 124 S.Ct. at 2372.   We reject the appellants' alternate theory and conclude that we are without subject-matter jurisdiction under the FTAIA.

While the FTAIA excludes from the Sherman Act's reach most anti-competitive conduct that causes only foreign injury, it creates exceptions for conduct that "significantly harms imports, domestic commerce, or American exporters." *Empagran*, 124 S.Ct. at 2363. At issue is the "domestic-injury exception" of section 6a(2), which we conclude, as counsel for the United States argued, applies in only limited circumstances.

The appellees suggest that the exception applies only to injuries that arise in U.S. commerce, thus describing its reach by the situs of the transaction and resulting injuries rather than by the situs of the effects of the allegedly anti-competitive conduct giving rise to the appellants' claims. This interpretation has no support from the text of the statute, which expressly covers conduct involving "trade or commerce with foreign nations." In addition, the legislative history makes clear that the FTAIA's "domestic effects" requirement "does not exclude all persons injured abroad from recovering under the antitrust laws of the United States." The appellants need only demonstrate therefore that the U.S. effects of the appellees' allegedly anti-competitive conduct "g[a]ve rise to" their claims.

During oral argument, counsel for the United States identified three decisions with factual scenarios that, in its view, satisfy the narrow "domestic-injury exception": *Pfizer, Inc. v. Gov't of India*, 434 U.S. 308 (1978); *Industria Siciliana Asfalti, Bitumi, S.p.A. v. Exxon Research & Eng'g Co.*, 1977 WL 1353 (S.D.N.Y.1977); and *Caribbean Broad. Sys. v. Cable & Wireless PLC*, 148 F.3d 1080 (D.C.Cir.1998). Counsel nonetheless argued, and we agree, that each of these cases is distinguishable. For example, in *Pfizer*, which involved a conspiracy that operated both domestically and internationally, the Supreme Court held "only that a foreign nation otherwise entitled to sue in our courts is entitled to sue for treble damages under the antitrust laws to the same extent as any other plaintiff," without addressing the requisite causal relationship between domestic effect and foreign injury. In *Industria*, the foreign injury was "inextricably bound up with the domestic restraints of trade," because a reciprocal tying agreement effected the exclusion of the American rival of one defendant, resulting in higher consumer prices. Finally, in *Caribbean* this court expressly found the FTAIA permitted a Sherman Act claim that involved solely foreign injury. There the plaintiff broadcaster, Caribbean, which operated an FM radio station based in the British Virgin Islands, filed an antitrust action against a competing FM radio station and its joint venturer, alleging that the defendants had violated the Sherman Act by preserving the defendant station's radio broadcast monopoly in the eastern Caribbean region through, *inter alia,* misrepresentations to its advertisers regarding the station's broadcasting reach. While the court expressly addressed only how Caribbean's allegations satisfied subsection 1 of the FTAIA (finding the requisite effect of the defendants' conduct on domestic trade or commerce), it is clear from the court's opinion that Caribbean's allegations satisfied subsection 2 as well. The domestic effect the court found was that U.S. advertisers paid the defendant station excessive prices for advertising. It was this effect of the defendants' monopolizing conduct -- forcing U.S. businesses to pay for advertising on the defendant station - that caused Caribbean to lose revenue because it was unable to sell advertising to the same U.S. businesses. *See* 148 F.3d at 1087.

> The appellants' theory in a nutshell is as follows:
> Because the appellees' product (vitamins) was fungible and globally marketed, they were able to sustain super-competitive prices abroad only by maintaining super-competitive prices in the United States as well.[86] Otherwise, overseas purchasers would have purchased bulk vitamins at lower prices either directly from U.S. sellers or from arbitrageurs selling vitamins imported from the United States, thereby preventing the appellees from selling abroad at the inflated prices. Thus, the super-competitive pricing in the United States "gives rise to" the foreign super-competitive prices from which the appellants claim injury.

The appellants paint a plausible scenario under which maintaining super-competitive prices in the United States might well have been a

---

[86] The appellants assert the appellees accomplished this equipoise both by fixing a single global price for the vitamins and by creating barriers to international vitamin commerce in the form of market division agreements that prevented bulk vitamins from being traded between North America and other regions.

"but-for" cause of the appellants' foreign injury. As the appellants acknowledged at oral argument, however, "but-for" causation between the domestic effects and the foreign injury claim is simply not sufficient to bring anti-competitive conduct within the FTAIA exception. The statutory language - "gives rise to" - indicates a direct causal relationship, that is, proximate causation, and is not satisfied by the mere but-for "nexus" the appellants advanced in their brief. *See* Appellants Br. at 22-23. This interpretation of the statutory language accords with principles of "prescriptive comity" - "the respect sovereign nations afford each other by limiting the reach of their laws," *Hartford Fire Ins. Co. v. California,* 509 U.S. 764, 817 (1993) (Scalia, J., dissenting) - which require that we "ordinarily construe[] ambiguous statutes to avoid unreasonable interference with the sovereign authority of other nations." *F. Hoffman-La Roche, Ltd.,* 124 S.Ct. at 2366. To read the FTAIA broadly to permit a more flexible, less direct standard than proximate cause would open the door to just such interference with other nations' prerogative to safeguard their own citizens from anti-competitive activity within their own borders. *See id.* at 2367 ("Why should American law supplant, for example, Canada's or Great Britain's or Japan's own determination about how best to protect Canadian or British or Japanese customers from anticompetitive conduct engaged in [in] significant part by Canadian or British or Japanese or other foreign companies?").

Applying the proximate cause standard, we conclude the domestic effects the appellants cite did not give rise to their claimed injuries so as to bring their Sherman Act claim within the FTAIA exception. While maintaining super-competitive prices in the United States may have facilitated the appellees' scheme to charge comparable prices abroad, this fact demonstrates at most but-for causation. It does not establish, as in the cases the United States cites, that the U.S. effects of the appellees' conduct - i.e., increased prices in the United States - proximately caused the foreign appellants' injuries. Nor do the appellants otherwise identify the kind of direct tie to U.S. commerce found in the cited cases. Although the appellants argue that the vitamin market is a single, global market facilitated by market division agreements so that their injuries arose from the higher prices charged by the global conspiracy (rather than from super-competitive prices in one particular market), they still must satisfy the FTAIA's

135

requirement that the U.S. effects of the conduct give rise to their claims. The but-for causation the appellants proffer establishes only an indirect connection between the U.S. prices and the prices they paid when they purchased vitamins abroad. *Cf. Sniado v. Bank Austria AG,* 378 F.3d 210, 213 (2d. Cir.2004). Under the appellants' theory, it was the foreign effects of price-fixing outside of the United States that directly caused, or "g[a]ve rise to," their losses when they purchased vitamins abroad at super-competitive prices. That the appellees knew or could foresee the effect of their allegedly anti-competitive activities in the United States on the appellants' injuries abroad or had as a purpose to manipulate United States trade does not establish that "U.S. effects" proximately caused the appellants' harm. The foreign injury caused by the appellees' conduct, then, was not "inextricably bound up with . . . domestic restraints of trade," as in *Industria* and *Caribbean Broadcasting. See Empagran,* 124 S.Ct. at 2370. It was the foreign effects of price-fixing outside of the United States that directly caused or "g[a]ve rise to" the appellants' losses when they purchased vitamins abroad at super-competitive prices.

For the foregoing reasons, the judgment of the district court is affirmed.